FRENCH
COOKING

FRENCH COOKING

General Editor JENI WRIGHT
Author ELISABETH SCOTTO

LANGHAM PRESS

CONTENTS

Original recipes written by Elisabeth Scotto

Translated by Jeni Wright

First published 1983 by Langham Press,
Langham Park, Catteshall Lane,
Godalming, Surrey
in association with Octopus Books Limited,
59 Grosvenor Street, London W1

© Octopus Books Limited 1983

ISBN 0 86362 010 8

Produced by Mandarin Publishers Limited,
22a Westlands Road, Quarry Bay, Hong Kong

Printed in Hong Kong

Introduction

France enjoys the reputation of having not one, but two, of the finest cuisines in the world. *La haute cuisine* was established by famous chefs such as La Varenne, Carême and Escoffier and is continued today by leading chefs in some of the world's most celebrated restaurants. In contrast, *la cuisine regionale* developed from a basic need to utilize the land's varied produce efficiently – and this still remains predominant in homes and restaurants, inns and cafes throughout France. From this style of cooking have evolved many of the famous regional specialities featured in the following pages, so here we explain how the regions differ in terms of readily available ingredients.

The North: Flanders, Artois, Picardy. The traditional home of coal-mining and the textile and metalurgical industries, it also produces one-fifth of French sugar as well as corn, wheat, rye and potatoes. The cooking is simple but hearty, with strong flavours predominating. Leeks, chicory (endive), red and white cabbage, potatoes and dried haricot beans are favourite foods; frogs' legs and eels are also popular, as is fresh fish . . . on the Channel coast is France's largest fishing port, Boulogne-sur-Mer.

The North-East: Alsace, Lorraine, Champagne, Franche-Comté, Ile de France. Probably the most productive and varied of all the areas of France, Alsace has rich plains for cereals and vegetables, fields of cattle, vine-clad hillsides, orchards, forests rich in game, and innumerable rivers teeming with fish. Many dishes are Germanic in character – nearby Germany has dominated the region in the past – but also evident is the influence of its Jewish colonies. Smoked foods are popular, as is *choucroute* (Alsatian sauerkraut). *Foie gras* is the most famous speciality. Lorraine is similarly fertile, but is most famous for the *quiche* which bears its name. Champagne's rivers are rich with eel, pike, perch, carp and trout – the area originated *truites aux amandos*; and the world-famous sparkling wine is produced here. Franche-Comté is a small region of plateaux, plains and mountains, and its pride is the cattle whose rich milk is turned into thick cream and a delectable cheese – *Gruyère de Comté*. Ile de France covers Paris and the surrounding departments, and is outstanding for its culinary successes: *entrecôte Bercy* (entrecôte steaks with *beurre Bercy*), *soupe à l'oignon gratinée* (onion soup with crusty bread and cheese topping), patisserie such as *éclairs, profiteroles* and the superb *gâteau Saint-Honoré*, all filled with *crème pâtissière* or *crème Chantilly*.

The North West: Normandy, Brittany, Vendée. Notable for delicious but surprisingly simple dishes. Normandy, largely coastal, is rich in dairy foods and farm poultry, but best known for its apples and the cider and *calvados* (apple brandy) made from them. Brittany has both the sea and rivers to provide a wonderful range of fish and shellfish used in hearty soups and stews. Lamb and mutton are highly prized too. Brittany is also known for *beurre blanc*, a salted butter sauce served with fish, and paper-thin *crêpes* (*galettes*) served sprinkled with salt, sugar or liqueur, or spread with jam or honey. Vendée enjoys a varied cuisine, seafood being the predominant feature.

The Loire Country: Orléanais, Touraine, Anjou, Maine. These large and fertile regions have market gardens, fruit farms and vineyards. Shallots (scallions) are used in most savoury dishes, and cream and butter are everyday ingredients. Potted and preserved meats (such as *rillettes de porc*) and *pâtés* are specialities.

The Centre: Berry, Auvergne, Limousin. An area of volcanic plateaux where the cooking is rustic and solid, relying largely on locally produced vegetables and mushrooms. Freshwater fish are plentiful, as are geese and chickens, and sheep are reared for meat and milk from which many excellent cheeses are made. Walnuts and chestnuts form the basis of many dishes and desserts.

The Rhône-Alps: Bourgogne, Lyonnais, Dauphiné, Savoie. Better known as Burgundy, *Bourgogne* is famous for its wines and tender beef from Charolais cattle. The two are combined to produce the excellent *boeuf bourguignon*. Dijon, one of the main towns, is world-renowned for its mustard and spice cakes. Lyonnais ranks with Paris as a great gastronomic centre. Truffles are one of the wonders of this cuisine; frogs, snails and freshwater fish are widely used; and pork provides *charcuterie* of superb quality. The most common dessert is the *beignet*, a sweet deep-fried fritter. Blackcurrants are used in many desserts and for the famous liqueur, *cassis*. Dauphiné and Savoie, mountainous regions on the borders of Italy and Switzerland, have abundant carp, crayfish and trout; good pastures produce excellent butter, cream and cheeses, and many varieties of mushroom. For desserts, dried fruits and nuts are favoured.

Aquitaine: Bordeaux, Périgord, Gascoigne, Béarn. This area, on the Bay of Biscay, is the link between France and Spain. It has a rich and varied cuisine, but Périgord is perhaps the best known, because truffles and cèpes mushrooms are found here. Geese are bred for *foie gras*, and an enormous range of *charcuterie* is available. Cultivated snails fatten on leaves from the vines which produce the grapes eventually made into Bordeaux wines.

The South: Toulouse, Languedoc, Roussillon, Provence, Côte d'Azur. The position of Toulouse, bordering onto the Pyrenees, ensures a plentiful supply of fish, but the traditional, best known dish of the region is *cassoulet*. The region also has plentiful fruit and vegetables, truffles and *foie gras*. Languedoc-Roussillon borders the Mediterranean and includes Sète, where there is a large-scale fishing industry. Olive trees grow in profusion, producing the strong-flavoured cooking oil indispensable to the south-east. The region's cuisine is rich in fish and shellfish, mutton and suckling kid, fruit and vegetables. The people of Provence are essentially Mediterranean rather than French and have a language of their own. Local agriculture is intensive; fruit and vegetables grow in abundance. Rice grows in the Camargue and The Crau plain supplies the whole region with meat and milk. As in Languedoc, Provençal dishes are heady with the flavour and aroma of olive oil, garlic and herbs. Along the coast, the prolific fish and shellfish are either grilled or used in magnificent fish soups and stews.

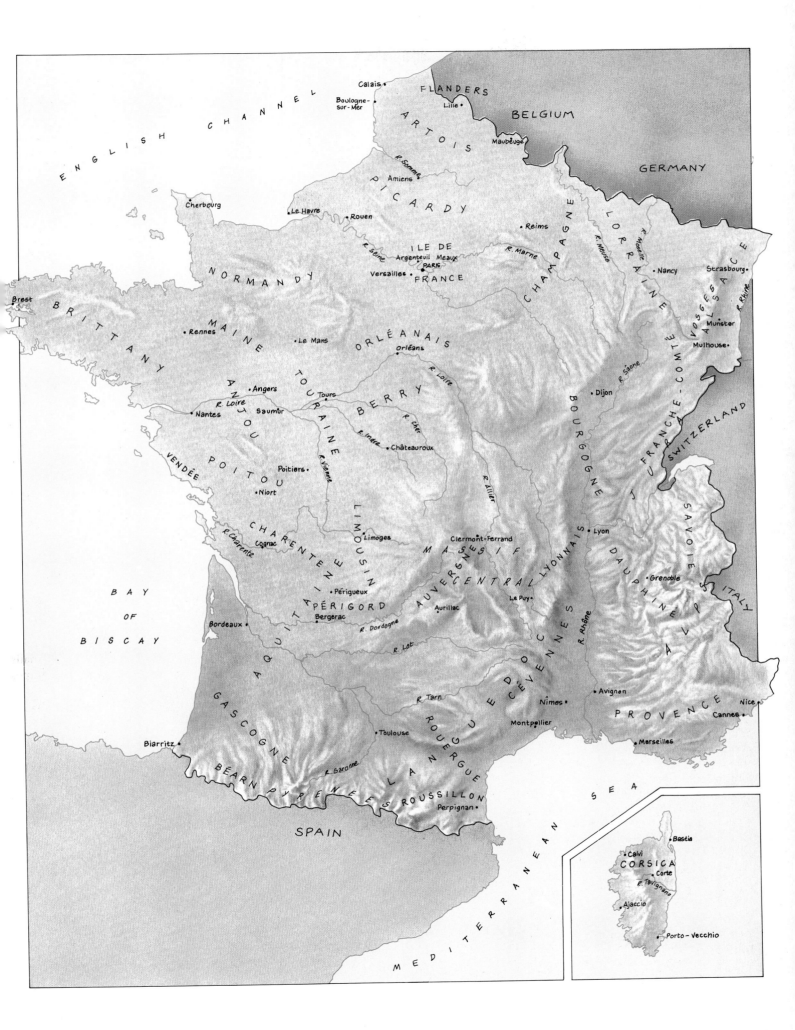

BASIC RECIPES

BOUILLON DE VIANDE
Meat Stock

This basic meat stock can be used in any recipe calling for 'beef stock'. For a richer 'brown' stock, a must for classic sauces such as demi-glace and espagnole, the meat and bones should first be browned in the pan in a little hot dripping, or roasted in a hot oven (220°C/425°F/Gas Mark 7) for 30 to 40 minutes. After browning, proceed with the recipe as below. Some recipes which are both delicate in flavour and colour call for 'light' or veal stock. This is made in exactly the same way as beef stock, but using a knuckle of veal and pieces of shin, breast or shoulder of veal instead of the beef. After straining meat stocks, do not discard the meat — it can be chopped or minced (ground) and used for making meatballs and stuffings, etc.

Metric/Imperial	American
2 carrots, peeled and roughly chopped	2 carrots, peeled and roughly chopped
2 celery sticks, roughly chopped	2 celery stalks, roughly chopped
2 leeks, roughly chopped	2 leeks, roughly chopped
750 g/1½ lb flank or shin of beef, cut into large chunks	1½ lb flank or shin of beef, cut into large chunks
450 g/1 lb knuckle of veal, cut into large chunks	1 lb knuckle of veal, cut into large chunks
1 calf's foot★, chopped (optional)	1 calf's foot★, chopped (optional)
1 onion, peeled and stuck with 2 whole cloves	1 onion, peeled and stuck with 2 whole cloves
1 bouquet garni★	1 bouquet garni★
6 black peppercorns	6 black peppercorns
salt	salt
3 litres/5½ pints water	6½ pints/13 cups water

Put the vegetables, except the onion, in the bottom of a large pan. Place the beef, veal and calf's foot (if using) on top. Add the onion, bouquet garni, peppercorns and salt to taste.

Pour in the water and bring slowly to the boil. Lower the heat, skim off the scum with a slotted spoon, then half-cover with a lid. Simmer for 3 hours, skimming off the scum again after the first 15 minutes and topping up the water during cooking if the liquid falls below the level of the meats.

Leave to cool, then remove the beef, veal and calf's foot (if used). Tip the vegetables and liquid into a sieve or fine colander lined with muslin (cheesecloth) wrung out in hot water. Press firmly to extract as much stock as possible.

Leave the stock until completely cold, then remove the fat that has risen to the surface. Store covered in the refrigerator for up to 4 days, or in the freezer for up to 3 months. Bring to the boil before using as required.
MAKES ABOUT 1.5 litres/2½ pints/6¼ cups

BOUILLON DE VOLAILLE
Chicken Stock

Eat the chicken from this stock hot as a main course with vegetables, or leave until cold, then slice, chop or mince (grind) and use in salads or made-up dishes.

Metric/Imperial	American
2 carrots, peeled and roughly chopped	2 carrots, peeled and roughly chopped
2 celery sticks, roughly chopped	2 celery stalks, roughly chopped
2 leeks, roughly chopped	2 leeks, roughly chopped
1 × 1.5 kg/3–3½ lb chicken, with giblets	1 × 3–3½ lb chicken, with giblets
1 calf's foot★, chopped (optional)	1 calf's foot★, chopped (optional)
1 onion, peeled and stuck with 2 whole cloves	1 onion, peeled and stuck with 2 whole cloves
1 bouquet garni★	1 bouquet garni★
6 black peppercorns	6 black peppercorns
salt	salt
3 litres/5½ pints water	6½ pints/13 cups water

Put the vegetables, except the onion, in the bottom of a large pan. Place the chicken on top of the vegetables with the giblets, calf's foot (if using), onion, bouquet garni, peppercorns and salt to taste.

Pour in the water and bring slowly to the boil. Skim off the scum with a slotted spoon, then lower the heat and half-cover with a lid. Simmer for 3 hours, skimming off the scum again after the first 15 minutes and topping up the water during the cooking time if it falls below the level of the chicken.

Leave to cool, then remove the chicken, giblets and calf's foot (if used). Tip the vegetables and liquid into a sieve or fine colander lined with muslin (cheesecloth) wrung out in hot water. Press firmly to extract as much stock as possible.

Leave the stock until completely cold, then remove the fat that has risen to the surface. Store covered in the refrigerator for up to 4 days, or in the freezer for up to 3 months. Bring to the boil before using as required.
MAKES ABOUT 1.5 litres/2½ pints/6¼ cups

FUMET DE POISSON
Fish Stock

Do not use oily fish for making this stock or it will have too strong a flavour. Cod, halibut and plaice are ideal, so too are turbot and sole, which will make the stock rich and gelatinous. Dry white wine, if available, can be used to replace some of the water to give the stock extra flavour.

Metric/Imperial	American
1 kg/2 lb white fish trimmings (including heads and bones)	2 lb white fish trimmings (including heads and bones)
1 large onion, peeled and sliced	1 large onion, peeled and sliced
1 large carrot, peeled and sliced	1 large carrot, peeled and sliced
2 celery sticks, roughly chopped	2 celery stalks, roughly chopped
1.75 litres/3 pints water	3¾ pints/7½ cups water
2 tablespoons lemon juice	2 tablespoons lemon juice
1 bouquet garni★	1 bouquet garni★
6 white peppercorns	6 white peppercorns
1 teaspoon salt	1 teaspoon salt

Put all the ingredients in a large pan and bring slowly to the boil. Lower the heat and skim off the scum with a slotted spoon. Simmer uncovered for 30 minutes, skimming off the scum again during this time, if necessary.

Tip the contents of the pan into a sieve or fine colander lined with muslin (cheesecloth) wrung out in hot water. Press firmly to extract as much stock as possible.

Leave the stock until completely cold. Cover and store in the refrigerator for up to 2 days. Use as required.

MAKES ABOUT 1.5 litres/2½ pints/6¼ cups

BOUILLON DE LEGUMES
Vegetable Stock

For use in vegetarian dishes and in delicately flavoured sauces and vegetable cream soups, etc., when the flavour of meat or poultry stock would be too strong.

Metric/Imperial	American
25 g/1 oz butter	2 tablespoons butter
450 g/1 lb onions, peeled and sliced	1 lb onions, peeled and sliced
450 g/1 lb carrots, peeled and sliced	1 lb carrots, peeled and sliced
1 head celery, with the leaves, roughly chopped	1 head celery, with the leaves, roughly chopped
1.75 litres/3 pints water	3¾ pints/7½ cups water
1 bouquet garni★	1 bouquet garni★
6 white peppercorns	6 white peppercorns
½ teaspoon salt	½ teaspoon salt

Melt the butter in a large pan, add the vegetables and fry gently until softened, stirring frequently. Do not allow the vegetables to become browned or this will spoil the colour of the finished stock.

Stir in the water, then add the remaining ingredients and bring slowly to the boil. Lower the heat, skim off any scum with a slotted spoon, then half-cover with a lid. Simmer for 1 to 2 hours. Top up the water during the cooking time if the liquid reduces in the pan.

Tip the contents of the pan into a sieve or fine colander lined with muslin (cheesecloth) wrung out in hot water. Press firmly to extract as much stock as possible.

Leave the stock until completely cold. Cover and store in the refrigerator for up to 5 days, or in the freezer for up to 3 months. Bring to the boil before using as required.

MAKES ABOUT 1.5 litres/2½ pints/6¼ cups

SAUCE BÉCHAMEL

*This basic white coating sauce is used in numerous different
ways – on its own, as a base for other sauces, in gratin dishes
and quiches, etc.*

Metric/Imperial	American
50 g/2 oz butter	¼ cup butter
50 g/2 oz plain flour	½ cup all-purpose flour
500 ml/18 fl oz hot milk	2¼ cups hot milk
salt	salt
freshly ground white pepper	freshly ground white pepper
freshly grated nutmeg	freshly grated nutmeg

Melt the butter in a heavy pan, sprinkle in the flour and
cook, stirring constantly, for 1 minute to obtain a
smooth *roux* (paste). Remove from the heat.

Pour the milk into the pan a little at a time, stirring
vigorously after each addition to allow the *roux* to
absorb the milk without forming lumps.

Bring slowly to the boil, stirring constantly, then
lower the heat and simmer for 5 to 6 minutes until the
sauce thickens, stirring frequently.

Add salt, pepper and nutmeg to taste, then remove
from the heat. Use immediately.
MAKES ABOUT 600 ml/1 pint/2½ cups

NOTE: For extra flavour, add chopped parsley, chervil
or tarragon to taste.

Sauce crème: After making the béchamel sauce,
whisk in 25 g/1 oz/2 tablespoons softened butter,
200 ml/⅓ pint/1 cup double (heavy) cream and 1 teaspoon lemon juice. Serve with plain-boiled vegetables
or roast chicken.

SAUCE MORNAY

Cheese Sauce

*This sauce has a pouring consistency, and is most often
served with vegetables and fish.*

Metric/Imperial	American
25 g/1 oz butter	2 tablespoons butter
25 g/1 oz plain flour	¼ cup all-purpose flour
500 ml/18 fl oz hot milk	2¼ cups hot milk
salt	salt
freshly ground white pepper	freshly ground white pepper
freshly grated nutmeg	freshly grated nutmeg
100 g/4 oz Gruyère cheese★, grated	1 cup grated Gruyère cheese★
1 egg yolk	1 egg yolk
4 tablespoons double cream	¼ cup heavy cream

Make a béchamel sauce (as above) with the butter,
flour, milk and salt, pepper and nutmeg to taste.

Add the cheese a little at a time, over the lowest
possible heat, stirring vigorously with a wooden spoon
until the cheese melts.

Put the egg yolk in a bowl and whisk with a fork.
Whisk in the cream gradually, then stir into the sauce a
little at a time.

Reheat very gently whisking all the time; do not
allow the sauce to boil at this stage or it will separate
and become lumpy. Use immediately.
MAKES ABOUT 600 ml/1 pint/2½ cups

SAUCE SOUBISE

Onion Sauce

*This onion sauce is used for coating fish and meat dishes. It
is also a classic accompaniment to gigot à la bretonne (leg of
lamb with haricot (navy) beans page 71)*

Metric/Imperial	American
75 g/3 oz butter, softened	⅓ cup softened butter
225 g/8 oz onions, peeled and thinly sliced	½ lb onions, peeled and thinly sliced
7 tablespoons double cream	7 tablespoons heavy cream
BÉCHAMEL SAUCE:	BÉCHAMEL SAUCE:
50 g/2 oz butter	¼ cup butter
50 g/2 oz plain flour	½ cup all-purpose flour
500 ml/18 fl oz hot milk	2¼ cups hot milk
salt	salt
freshly ground white pepper	freshly ground white pepper
freshly grated nutmeg	freshly grated nutmeg

Melt 25 g/1 oz/2 tablespoons butter in a heavy pan, add
the onions and fry very gently for 30 minutes until soft
and golden, stirring frequently.

Meanwhile, make a béchamel sauce (see opposite)
with the butter, flour, milk, and salt, pepper and
nutmeg to taste.

Stir the béchamel sauce into the onions, cover the
pan and simmer very gently for 15 minutes, stirring
from time to time.

Work the onion sauce through a fine sieve (strainer)
into a clean pan, rubbing vigorously. Bring slowly to
just below boiling point, stirring constantly, then
remove from the heat.

Stir the cream into the sauce, then whisk in the
remaining softened butter a little at a time. Taste and
adjust seasoning. Serve immediately.
MAKES ABOUT 600 ml/1 pint/2½ cups

SAUCE MOUTARDE

Mustard Sauce

*A coating sauce to serve with veal escalopes, pork and veal
chops and vegetables.*

Metric/Imperial	American
50 g/2 oz butter	¼ cup butter
50 g/2 oz plain flour	½ cup all-purpose flour
500 ml/18 fl oz hot milk	2¼ cups hot milk
salt	salt
freshly ground white pepper	freshly ground white pepper
1 onion, peeled and stuck with 1 clove (optional)	1 onion, peeled and stuck with 1 clove (optional)
150 ml/¼ pint double cream	⅔ cup heavy cream
3 tablespoons prepared French mustard★	3 tablespoons prepared French mustard★
dash of red wine vinegar	dash of red wine vinegar

Make a béchamel sauce (see opposite) with the butter,
flour, milk, and salt and pepper to taste.

Add the onion (if using) and simmer very gently for
30 minutes, stirring frequently.

Remove the onion from the sauce, then stir in the
cream, mustard and wine vinegar. Bring back to the
boil, stirring constantly, then taste and adjust seasoning. Use immediately.
MAKES ABOUT 750 ml/1¼ pints/3 cups

SAUCE HOLLANDAISE

To accompany cooked fish dishes and vegetables, particularly asparagus and boiled new potatoes. In this recipe the finished sauce is passed through a strainer before serving, to remove any particles of pepper and make the sauce extra smooth. This process is not absolutely necessary if time is short.

Metric/Imperial	American
225 g/8 oz butter, cut into small pieces	1 cup butter, cut into small pieces
2 tablespoons white wine vinegar	2 tablespoons white wine vinegar
4 tablespoons water	$\frac{1}{4}$ cup water
$\frac{1}{4}$–$\frac{1}{2}$ teaspoon freshly ground white pepper, according to taste	$\frac{1}{4}$–$\frac{1}{2}$ teaspoon freshly ground white pepper, according to taste
3 egg yolks	3 egg yolks
1–2 tablespoons lemon juice	1–2 tablespoons lemon juice
salt	salt

To clarify the butter: put the butter in a heavy pan and melt over very low heat. Skim off the white foam that rises to the surface, then strain the clear yellow liquid into a bowl, leaving behind the milky residue.

Put the vinegar in a heavy pan with 2 tablespoons water, and pepper to taste. Boil rapidly until the liquid has reduced to 1 teaspoon. Remove from the heat, then stand the pan in a hot *bain marie*★.

Stir 1 tablespoon water into the reduced liquid, then add the egg yolks one at a time, whisking vigorously after each addition.

Whisk in the clarified butter a little at a time, then whisk in the remaining water. The consistency of the sauce should be like thick cream at this stage.

Pass the sauce through a *chinois* then whisk in the lemon juice and salt to taste. Serve immediately.

4 SERVINGS

Sauce mousseline: Fold 2 tablespoons lightly whipped cream into the hollandaise sauce just before serving.

SAUCE BÉARNAISE

To accompany all grilled (broiled) steaks and roast beef.

Metric/Imperial	American
225 g/8 oz butter, cut into small pieces	1 cup butter, cut into small pieces
7 tablespoons white wine vinegar	7 tablespoons white wine vinegar
2 shallots, peeled and very finely chopped	2 scallions, peeled and very finely chopped
$\frac{1}{4}$–$\frac{1}{2}$ teaspoon freshly ground white pepper, according to taste	$\frac{1}{4}$–$\frac{1}{2}$ teaspoon freshly ground white pepper, according to taste
2 tablespoons chopped tarragon	2 tablespoons chopped tarragon
3 egg yolks	3 egg yolks
2 tablespoons water	2 tablespoons water
salt	salt

To clarify the butter: put the butter in a heavy pan and melt over very low heat. Skim off the white foam that rises to the surface, then strain the clear yellow liquid into a bowl, leaving behind the milky residue.

Put the vinegar in a heavy pan with the shallots (scallions), pepper to taste and half the tarragon. Boil rapidly until the liquid has reduced to 1 tablespoon.

Rub the reduced liquid through a fine sieve (strainer) into a clean pan, then stand the pan in a hot *bain marie*★.

Add the egg yolks to the strained liquid one at a time, whisking vigorously after each addition. Whisk in the water.

Whisk in the clarified butter a little at a time until the consistency of the sauce is like thick cream. Add the remaining tarragon and salt to taste. Serve immediately.

4 SERVINGS

Sauce choron: Substitute tomato purée (paste) for the 2 tablespoons of tarragon and whisk it in at the end of making the béarnaise sauce. The quantity can vary from 1 to 4 tablespoons, according to taste.

SAUCE VELOUTÉ

One of the classic French sauces, which can be served on its own like béchamel sauce, or used as a base for other classic sauces.

Metric/Imperial	American
100 g/4 oz butter	*½ cup butter*
25 g/1 oz plain flour	*¼ cup all-purpose flour*
500 ml/18 fl oz hot chicken stock (page 8)	*2¼ cups hot chicken stock (page 8)*
salt	*salt*
freshly ground white pepper	*freshly ground white pepper*

To clarify the butter: put half of the butter in a heavy pan and melt over very low heat. Skim off the white foam that rises to the surface, then strain the clear yellow liquid into a clean pan, leaving behind the milky residue.

Place over low heat again, sprinkle in the flour and cook, stirring constantly, for 2 minutes.

Stir in the hot stock a little at a time, whisking vigorously after each addition. Bring slowly to the boil, stirring constantly, then stand over the lowest possible heat and simmer very gently for 1 hour, stirring occasionally. Skim the sauce with a slotted spoon from time to time to remove any impurities and fat that rise to the surface.

Remove from the heat, then work through a fine sieve (strainer) into a clean pan. Reheat very gently, then remove from the heat and whisk in the remaining butter a little at a time until thoroughly incorporated. Add salt and pepper to taste. Serve immediately.
MAKES ABOUT 600 ml/1 pint/2½ cups

NOTE: If the sauce is not to be served immediately, make it up to the sieving stage, then leave to cool. Reheat and add the butter just before serving – once the butter is added the sauce will not keep.

SAUCE VERTE

Piquant Green Sauce

This 'green sauce' is served as an accompaniment to grilled (broiled) fish and meat, the meat from a pot-au-feu (page 68) and boiled salt pork.

Metric/Imperial	American
1 tablespoon wine vinegar	*1 tablespoon wine vinegar*
salt	*salt*
freshly ground black pepper	*freshly ground black pepper*
2 tablespoons chopped parsley	*2 tablespoons chopped parsley*
1 tablespoon chopped chervil	*1 tablespoon chopped chervil*
1 tablespoon snipped chives	*1 tablespoon snipped chives*
1 tablespoon very finely chopped capers	*1 tablespoon very finely chopped capers*
6 small gherkins, very finely chopped	*6 small sweet dill pickles, very finely chopped*
2 shallots, peeled and very finely chopped	*2 scallions, peeled and very finely chopped*
4 tablespoons olive oil	*¼ cup olive oil*

Put the vinegar in a bowl with salt and pepper to taste. Add the remaining ingredients, except the oil; stir well.

Pour in the oil in a steady stream, whisking vigorously with a fork until all the oil is incorporated. Pour into a sauceboat and serve cold.
4 SERVINGS

VARIATIONS: Other ingredients can be added to this sauce, according to taste – very finely chopped canned anchovies (drained and desalted★), very finely chopped hard-boiled (cooked) egg and crushed garlic are just a few suggestions. Mint, tarragon or basil can be substituted for some of the herbs, or mixed with them according to availability. If a thicker sauce is liked, whisk in a few tablespoons of fresh breadcrumbs.

SAUCE TOMATE

This is just one of the many variations of tomato sauce to be found in French cooking – each region has its own favourite.

Metric/Imperial	**American**
50 g/2 oz goose fat★, or 4 tablespoons olive oil	¼ cup goose fat★ or olive oil
2 large onions, peeled and finely chopped	2 large onions, peeled and finely chopped
4 garlic cloves, peeled and crushed	4 garlic cloves, peeled and crushed
1 kg/2 lb ripe tomatoes, skinned, seeded and crushed	4 cups skinned, seeded and crushed tomatoes
1 tablespoon tomato purée	1 tablespoon tomato paste
¼–½ teaspoon sugar	¼–½ teaspoon sugar
1 bouquet garni★	1 bouquet garni★
salt	salt
freshly ground black pepper	freshly ground black pepper
freshly grated nutmeg	freshly grated nutmeg
chopped parsley	chopped parsley

Heat the fat or oil in a heavy pan, add the onions and garlic and fry gently for 15 minutes, stirring often.

Add the tomatoes, tomato purée (paste), sugar, bouquet garni, and salt, pepper and nutmeg to taste. Bring to the boil, then lower the heat, cover and simmer gently for 45 minutes, stirring occasionally.

Remove from the heat and discard the bouquet garni. Taste and adjust seasoning, then add parsley to taste. Serve hot.

MAKES ABOUT 450 ml/¾ pint/2 cups

SAUCE POULETTE
Mushroom Sauce

This sauce is the traditional accompaniment to tripe, although it is also sometimes served with shellfish.

Metric/Imperial	**American**
25 g/1 oz butter	2 tablespoons butter
225 g/8 oz mushrooms, finely sliced	2–2½ cups finely sliced mushrooms
juice of 1 lemon	juice of 1 lemon
7 tablespoons double cream	7 tablespoons heavy cream
3 egg yolks	3 egg yolks
500 ml/18 fl oz chicken stock (page 8)	2¼ cups chicken stock (page 8)
1 tablespoon cornflour	1 tablespoon cornstarch
2 tablespoons water	2 tablespoons water
1 tablespoon chopped parsley	1 tablespoon chopped parsley
salt	salt
freshly ground white pepper	freshly ground white pepper

Melt the butter in a pan, add the mushrooms and lemon juice and cook over moderate heat for 15 minutes.

Meanwhile, put the cream in a bowl, add the egg yolks and whisk to combine

Bring the stock to the boil in a pan. Mix the cornflour (cornstarch) to a paste with the water, then stir into the stock and cook until beginning to thicken.

Whisk 3 tablespoons of the hot stock into the cream and egg yolk mixture, then pour this mixture gradu-ally into the stock in the pan, whisking vigorously all the time. Add the mushrooms and their cooking juices, the parsley and salt and pepper to taste.

Heat through gently over very low heat, whisking constantly; do not allow the sauce to boil or it will curdle. Serve immediately.

MAKES ABOUT 600 ml/1 pint/2½ cups

ROUILLE
Chilli Pepper and Garlic Sauce

This is the fiery hot sauce that is traditionally served with Bouillabaisse (page 46) in the Midi. Sometimes the breadcrumbs are replaced with a mashed or puréed boiled potato, and sometimes an egg yolk is used which makes the rouille more like a mayonnaise. Guests help themselves to rouille, which they stir into their bouillabaisse according to taste. It can be served with other fish soups, and is often spread like a paste on dried or toasted bread, then placed in the bottom of soup bowls before the soup is poured over. Rouille also makes an excellent accompaniment to grilled (broiled) fish, in which case, use water or milk in place of the fish stock.

Metric/Imperial	**American**
3 garlic cloves, peeled and halved	3 garlic cloves, peeled and halved
3 red chilli peppers, halved, cored and seeded	3 red chili peppers, halved, cored and seeded
1 thick slice bread, crust removed and crumbled	1 thick slice bread, crust removed and crumbled
1 tablespoon hot bouillabaisse stock or fish stock (page 9)	1 tablespoon hot bouillabaisse stock or fish stock (page 9)
200 ml/⅓ pint olive oil	1 cup olive oil
salt	salt

Put the garlic and chilli peppers in a mortar and pound to a paste with a pestle. Add the breadcrumbs and hot stock, then leave to stand for 1 minute.

Pound the mixture again until well mixed, then add the oil a drop at a time as when making mayonnaise. Pound constantly until all the oil is added and the sauce has become emulsified. Taste and add salt if necessary. Serve at room temperature, straight from the mortar.

6 SERVINGS

VINAIGRETTE
Oil and Vinegar Dressing

This is the basic recipe for vinaigrette, but there are many regional variations. For example, garlic and chopped fresh herbs are added in the south, fresh cream in Normandy.

Metric/Imperial	**American**
2 tablespoons wine vinegar	2 tablespoons wine vinegar
salt	salt
freshly ground black pepper	freshly ground black pepper
6 tablespoons olive oil	6 tablespoons olive oil

Put the vinegar in a bowl with salt and pepper to taste. Whisk with a fork, then add the oil and continue whisking until the dressing is thick. Taste and adjust seasoning.

MAKES ABOUT 120 ml/4 fl oz/½ cup

MAYONNAISE

This recipe is for the classic French mayonnaise made in a mortar and pestle, without mustard or other flavourings. If the flavour of mustard is liked, add ½ teaspoon prepared French mustard to the egg yolk before adding the oil; if left for 1 minute, this will also help the egg yolk and oil emulsify. A rotary beater or electric whisk can be used instead of the mortar and pestle, if this seems easier.

Metric/Imperial	American
1 egg yolk	*1 egg yolk*
120–150 ml/4–5 fl oz groundnut, corn or olive oil	*½–⅓ cup groundnut, corn or olive oil*
pinch of salt	*pinch of salt*
3–4 teaspoons white wine vinegar or lemon juice	*3–4 teaspoons white wine vinegar or lemon juice*

Have all equipment and ingredients at room temperature.

Put the egg yolk in a mortar and work with a pestle to break up the yolk.

Add the oil to the egg yolk a drop at a time, working together thoroughly before adding more oil.

When the mayonnaise begins to emulsify, add the oil faster and use the pestle more vigorously. The mayonnaise should be thick within 5 to 8 minutes.

Add salt to taste, then blend in the vinegar or lemon juice. Serve at room temperature, straight from the mortar.
MAKES ABOUT 150 ml/¼ pint/⅔ cup

AÏOLI

Garlic Mayonnaise

This is the very thick mayonnaise from Provence which is heavily laced with garlic (ail). It is often served with raw vegetables (crudités) at the start of a meal, but it also lends its name to le grand aïoli, an array of mixed meats, fish and vegetables served around a bowl of garlic mayonnaise, which is used as a dipping sauce. Aillade is a similar kind of provençal mayonnaise used to flavour the fish soups of the area – sometimes with chopped nuts added.

Metric/Imperial	American
5 garlic cloves, peeled and halved	*5 garlic cloves, peeled and halved*
1 thick slice white bread, soaked in milk	*1 thick slice white bread, soaked in milk*
2 egg yolks	*2 egg yolks*
pinch of salt	*pinch of salt*
250 ml/8 fl oz olive oil	*1 cup olive oil*
2 tablespoons lemon juice, or to taste	*2 tablespoons lemon juice, or to taste*
1–2 tablespoons boiling water	*1–2 tablespoons boiling water*

Pound the garlic in a mortar and pestle until well crushed. Squeeze the bread to extract as much milk as possible, then add to the garlic and pound again until a smooth purée is formed.

Add the egg yolks and salt and continue pounding until thoroughly incorporated and beginning to thicken.

Add the olive oil a drop at a time, as when making mayonnaise, adding it in a thin, steady stream as the mixture thickens. Continue pounding all the time to make a thick, smooth mayonnaise.

Stir in lemon juice to taste, then whisk in the boiling water to help 'set' the sauce – it should be very thick and heavy. Serve at room temperature.
MAKES ABOUT 450 ml/¾ pint/2 cups

SAUCE TARTARE

To accompany any cooked fish, meat or poultry dish. It is particularly good with 'spatch-cocked' chicken – the bird, usually a small poussin, is split down the back, secured with skewers, then grilled (broiled) or spit-roasted with melted butter.

Metric/Imperial	American
2 hard-boiled eggs	*2 hard-cooked eggs*
250 ml/8 fl oz olive oil	*1 cup olive oil*
1 tablespoon mayonnaise (opposite)	*1 tablespoon mayonnaise (opposite)*
1 teaspoon wine vinegar	*1 teaspoon wine vinegar*
1 tablespoon very finely chopped capers	*1 tablespoon very finely chopped capers*
6 small gherkins, very finely chopped	*6 small sweet dill pickles, very finely chopped*
1 tablespoon snipped chives	*1 tablespoon snipped chives*
salt	*salt*
freshly ground black pepper	*freshly ground black pepper*

Put the egg yolks in a bowl and mash with a fork to a smooth paste. Add the oil a drop at a time, whisking vigorously after each addition as for mayonnaise (opposite).

When all the oil is incorporated and the mixture is thick and creamy, whisk in the mayonnaise and vinegar, then the remaining ingredients with salt and pepper to taste. Serve cold.
6 SERVINGS

NOTE: For a sauce with more body, sieve the leftover egg whites and whisk into the sauce just before serving.

BEURRE BLANC

This butter sauce is the classic accompaniment to cooked fish dishes. The recipe is from Brittany, where more salted or slightly salted (semisweet) butter is used than in other regions of France. Most French cooks tend to use unsalted (sweet) butter in cooking, then add salt to taste before serving.

Metric/Imperial	American
4 medium shallots, peeled and very finely chopped	*4 medium scallions, peeled and very finely chopped*
150 ml/¼ pint dry white wine	*⅔ cup dry white wine*
7 tablespoons white wine vinegar	*7 tablespoons white wine vinegar*
225 g/8 oz slightly salted butter, chilled and diced	*1 cup semisweet butter, chilled and diced*
freshly ground white pepper	*freshly ground white pepper*

Put the shallots (scallions) in a heavy pan with the wine and wine vinegar. Boil rapidly until the liquid has reduced to about 1 tablespoon.

Transfer the liquid to a heatproof bowl and stand

over a pan of hot water. Add the chilled butter to the liquid, a piece at a time, whisking vigorously after each addition until the consistency of the mixture is like thick cream. Add pepper to taste.

Pour directly onto food or hand separately in a warmed sauceboat. Serve immediately.

5 TO 6 SERVINGS

NOTE: If a smooth sauce is liked, pour the sauce through a fine sieve (strainer) before serving.

BEURRE ROUGE

The classic red butter sauce to accompany grilled (broiled) steaks or roast beef. If roasting beef, make beurre rouge in the roasting pan: pour off any excess fat after roasting, then add the shallots (scallions) and wine etc. to the cooking juices and sediment in the pan and follow the recipe below.

Metric/Imperial	American
4 medium shallots, peeled and very finely chopped	*4 medium scallions, peeled and very finely chopped*
250 ml/8 fl oz red wine	*1 cup red wine*
1 tablespoon red wine vinegar	*1 tablespoon red wine vinegar*
salt	*salt*
freshly ground black pepper	*freshly ground black pepper*
225 g/8 oz unsalted butter, chilled and diced	*1 cup sweet butter, chilled and diced*

Put the shallots (scallions) in a heavy pan with the wine and wine vinegar, and salt and pepper to taste. Boil rapidly until the liquid has reduced to about 1 tablespoon.

Transfer the liquid to a heatproof bowl and stand over a pan of hot water. Add the chilled butter to the liquid, a piece at a time, whisking vigorously after each addition until the mixture is the consistency of thick cream. Taste and adjust seasoning.

Pour directly onto food or hand separately in a warmed sauceboat. Serve immediately.

5 TO 6 SERVINGS

NOTE: If a smooth sauce is liked, pour the sauce through a fine sieve (strainer) before serving.

BEURRE BERCY

This white butter with beef marrow is the classic accompaniment to grilled (broiled) steaks and roast beef.

Metric/Imperial	American
1 beef marrow bone★ (about 225 g/8 oz in weight)	1 beef marrow bone★ (about $\frac{1}{2}$ lb in weight)
salt	salt
2 shallots, peeled and very finely chopped	2 scallions, peeled and very finely chopped
200 ml/$\frac{1}{3}$ pint dry white wine	1 cup dry white wine
150 g/5 oz butter, softened	$\frac{2}{3}$ cup butter, softened
1 tablespoon lemon juice	1 tablespoon lemon juice
1 tablespoon chopped parsley	1 tablespoon chopped parsley
freshly ground black pepper	freshly ground black pepper

Split the marrow bone down the centre and take out the marrow. Chop it as finely as possible, using a knife dipped in hot water.

Drop the chopped marrow into a pan of boiling salted water, then lower the heat and simmer for 5 minutes until soft. Drain thoroughly.

Put the shallots (scallions) in a heavy pan with the wine and boil rapidly until reduced by half. Leave to cool.

Add the butter a little at a time to the reduced liquid, whisking vigorously after each addition, then whisk in the softened marrow a piece at a time. Add the lemon juice, parsley, and salt and pepper to taste, then whisk thoroughly to combine. The consistency of the butter should be like whipped cream. Serve cold on top of meat or hand separately in a serving bowl.

6 SERVINGS

BEURRE MARCHAND DE VIN

This butter is the classic accompaniment to entrecôte steak, but it can be served with any grilled (broiled) beef.

Metric/Imperial	American
3 shallots, peeled and very finely chopped	3 scallions, peeled and very finely chopped
200 ml/$\frac{1}{3}$ pint red wine	1 cup red wine
200 g/7 oz butter, softened	1 cup butter, softened
1 tablespoon lemon juice	1 tablespoon lemon juice
1 tablespoon chopped parsley	1 tablespoon chopped parsley
salt	salt
freshly ground black pepper	freshly ground black pepper

Put the shallots (scallions) in a heavy pan with the wine and boil rapidly until reduced by half. Leave to cool.

Add the butter a little at a time to the reduced liquid, whisking vigorously after each addition.

Add the lemon juice, parsley, and salt and pepper to taste, then whisk thoroughly to combine. The consistency of the butter should be like whipped cream.

Serve cold on top of meat or hand separately in a serving bowl.

6 SERVINGS

CRÈME ANGLAISE
Custard Sauce

This is the basic recipe for a custard sauce without flavourings, used either hot or cold for coating puddings and desserts when something a little less rich than fresh cream is required. If liked, infuse the milk with a vanilla pod (bean) before use, or add 1 teaspoon vanilla essence (extract) once the custard is cooked. 1 tablespoon liqueur can also be added for extra flavour, and melted chocolate can be stirred in to make a chocolate custard sauce for coating chocolate puddings.

Metric/Imperial	American
4 large egg yolks	4 large egg yolks
50–75 g/2–3 oz sugar, according to taste	$\frac{1}{4}$–$\frac{1}{3}$ cup sugar, according to taste
1 teaspoon cornflour	1 teaspoon cornstarch
450 ml/$\frac{3}{4}$ pint milk	2 cups milk

Put the egg yolks in a bowl with sugar to taste and whisk together until pale and thick. Whisk in the cornflour (cornstarch).

Bring the milk to just below boiling point, then gradually whisk into the egg yolk and sugar mixture.

Pour the custard into a heavy-based pan and stir over gentle heat with a wooden spoon until the custard begins to thicken and just coats the back of the spoon. Do not allow to boil or the custard will separate.

Remove from the heat, continue stirring for 1 to 2 minutes, then pour into a jug and serve immediately. To serve cold, cool quickly by transferring the sauce to a cold bowl, standing in a larger bowl of iced water. Stir continually until cold, then press a piece of cling film or greaseproof (wax) paper onto the surface of the sauce and chill in the refrigerator. Whisk vigorously before serving.

MAKES ABOUT 450 ml/$\frac{3}{4}$ pint/2 cups

CRÈME CHANTILLY
Chantilly Cream

Serve this cream either separately in a small bowl or pipe it attractively on desserts.

Metric/Imperial	American
250 ml/8 fl oz double cream, chilled	1 cup heavy cream, chilled
3 teaspoons caster sugar	3 teaspoons sugar

Whisk the cream in a cold basin until fluffy. Gradually add the sugar and continue to whisk slowly until the cream just holds its shape. Serve immediately.

MAKES ABOUT 250 ml/8 fl oz/1 cup

Crème chantilly aux Fruits can be made by doubling the basic recipe above and then adding 200 ml/$\frac{1}{3}$ pint/1 cup fresh strawberry or raspberry purée.

CRÈME FRAÎCHE

This cream is often used in France instead of sweet cream, especially in soups and fish and poultry dishes etc. as it adds more of a piquant flavour than ordinary double (heavy) cream. When first made, crème fraîche is sweet but on keeping it gradually acquires a tart flavour.

Metric/Imperial	American
250 ml/8 fl oz double cream	1 cup heavy cream
120 ml/4 fl oz soured cream	½ cup sour cream

Put both creams in a pan and stir well. Heat gently to 25°C/77°F (lukewarm). Pour cream into a jug and partly cover. Keep the cream at this warm temperature for 6 to 8 hours until thickened. Stir the cream then cover and refrigerate for up to 2 weeks.
MAKES ABOUT 350 ml/12 fl oz/1½ cups

CRÈME PÂTISSÌERE

Confectioner's Custard

So-called because of its use as a filling for all kinds of pâtisserie, crème patissière is a thick rich custard which sets on cooling to become quite firm. It is a popular filling for fruit flans and sweet tarts, and is also often used in choux buns and profiteroles. When crème pâtissière has beaten egg whites added to it, it is called crème Saint-Honoré.

Metric/Imperial	American
450 ml/¾ pint milk	2 cups milk
1 vanilla pod	1 vanilla bean
4 large egg yolks	4 large egg yolks
100 g/4 oz sugar	½ cup sugar
50 g/2 oz plain flour	½ cup all-purpose flour
knob of butter, to finish	knob of butter, to finish

Bring the milk to just below boiling point with the vanilla, then cover the pan and leave to infuse for 15 minutes. Strain, then bring to boiling point again.

Put the egg yolks in a bowl with the sugar and whisk together until pale and thick. Add the flour and whisk again until thoroughly incorporated, then gradually whisk in the boiling hot milk.

Pour the custard into a heavy-based pan and whisk over moderate heat until boiling. The mixture may be lumpy, in which case, remove from the heat and whisk vigorously until smooth. Return to the heat and bring to the boil again, then simmer for 1 to 2 minutes to cook the flour, whisking constantly.

Remove the custard from the heat, then rub the surface with the knob of butter to prevent a skin forming. Leave to cool before use.
MAKES ABOUT 450 ml/¾ pint/2 cups

PRALIN
Praline or Caramelized Almonds

In France, pralin is available ready-made from most pâtisseries, but if it is difficult for you to obtain, then it is quite easy to make at home and will keep for weeks in a screw-topped jar. Use it to sprinkle over ice cream and cream desserts and in icings, fillings and sauces.

Metric/Imperial	American
100 g/4 oz whole unblanched almonds	*¾ cup whole unblanched almonds*
100 g/4 oz sugar	*½ cup sugar*

Put the almonds and sugar in a heavy-based pan and stir over gentle heat until the sugar melts and caramelizes and the almonds are toasted.

Pour the mixture onto an oiled marble slab or baking sheet, then leave until completely cold and crisp.

Break the praline into pieces, then work in an electric grinder until pulverized to a fine powder, or pound in a mortar and pestle. Store in a screw-topped jar.

MAKES ABOUT 225 g/½ lb

PÂTE BRISÉE
Shortcrust Pastry (Basic Pie Dough)

A general-purpose pastry used for most savoury tarts and quiches, etc. For a richer pastry, add 2 egg yolks after cutting in the butter, then add less iced water to mix.

Metric/Imperial	American
225 g/8 oz plain flour	*2 cups all-purpose flour*
½ teaspoon salt	*½ teaspoon salt*
112 g/4 oz butter	*½ cup butter*
about 4 tablespoons iced water	*about ¼ cup iced water*

Sift the flour and salt into a bowl. Cut the butter into small pieces over the bowl then, with a round-bladed knife, cut it into the flour.

With the fingertips, rub the butter into the flour until the mixture resembles fine breadcrumbs. Work lightly, with hands held above the rim of the bowl to aerate the flour as much as possible to keep it light and short.

Stir in the water with the knife, adding it gradually until the mixture begins to draw together. With one hand, gather the dough together and form into a ball. Knead lightly until the dough is smooth and supple and free from cracks. Wrap in cling film or foil, then leave to relax in a cool place for 1 hour before use. In warm weather, chill in the refrigerator for 30 minutes, but allow to come to room temperature again before rolling out.

MAKES A '225 g/½ lb QUANTITY'

Pâte sucrée, or sweet shortcrust pastry (pie dough) is made exactly as for *pâte brisée* above, except that caster sugar is added to the flour before cutting in the butter. *Pâte sucrée* is used for sweet tarts and flans, and the amount of sugar varies according to individual recipes, from 25 g/1 oz/2 tablespoons to 100 g/4 oz/½ cup sugar for every 225 g/8 oz/2 cups flour.

Pâte sablée, commonly called French flan pastry, is a rich sweetened pastry used for flans and tarts which contain juicy fruits. It is made with the same ingredients as *pâte sucrée*, but enriched with egg yolks (2 to 4 egg yolks per 225 g/8 oz/2 cups flour according to individual recipes). It is more difficult to work than other less rich pastries, and is therefore usually mixed on a marble slab or other cold surface rather than in a bowl. It is easier to press it into the flan ring or pan rather than to roll it out on a floured board.

PÂTE À CHOUX
Choux Pastry

This is the basic recipe for choux pastry, used mostly in the making of choux buns, profiteroles and éclairs, but also in such recipes as the savoury cheese gougère de Bourgogne and the sumptuous gâteau Saint-Honoré.

Quantities of ingredients for making choux pastry vary considerably from one recipe to another, but you will notice that the proportions are always the same. It is therefore quite simple to use this basic method for recipes with different quantities.

Metric/Imperial	American
275 ml/½ pint water	*scant 1¼ cups water*
100 g/4 oz butter	*½ cup butter*
¾ teaspoon salt	*¾ teaspoon salt*
150 g/5 oz plain flour	*1¼ cups all-purpose flour*
about 4 large eggs	*about 4 large eggs*

Heat the water in a large pan with the butter and salt. When the butter has melted, bring the liquid to the boil and remove from the heat.

Immediately add the flour all at once, then beat vigorously with a wooden spoon. Return the pan to a low heat and continue beating until the mixture draws together and leaves the sides of the pan. Do not overbeat – the dough should be smooth and shiny, but not oily.

Remove the pan from the heat, then add the eggs one at a time, beating vigorously after each addition and making sure the egg is thoroughly incorporated before adding the next. Add the last egg a little at a time, beating to make a shiny dough that just falls from the spoon – if the dough will not absorb all the last egg, then do not add it.

For best results, use choux dough immediately, while still warm. If this is impossible, brush lightly with butter while still warm (to prevent a crust forming on its surface), leave until cool, then cover closely with greaseproof (wax) paper. Store in the refrigerator for up to 8 hours. To use, warm through in the pan on top of the stove, beating vigorously until smooth and shiny again.

MAKES A '4 EGG QUANTITY'

PÂTE FEUILLETÉE
Puff Pastry

Homemade puff pastry is far superior to its commercial frozen counterpart, but although not difficult to make, it is time-consuming. Remember always to work in the coolest conditions, with both cool hands and cool utensils, or the finished pastry will not be satisfactory. Puff pastry is very rich, with its equal weights of butter and flour. Similar but less rich pastries are rough puff and flaky, which use three-quarters fat to flour. Rough puff is the easiest of the three to make because the butter is simply stirred into the flour in pieces; in flaky pastry the butter is 'flaked' over the dough. All three pastries use the same rolling, folding and turning technique. For a puff pastry which is less rich, use only two-thirds of the butter specified here; this will also make it easier to handle.

Metric/Imperial	American
450 g/1 lb strong white flour	4 cups strong white (bread) flour
½ teaspoon salt	½ teaspoon salt
450 g/1 lb unsalted butter, chilled but not hard	2 cups sweet butter, chilled but not hard
2 teaspoons lemon juice (optional)	2 teaspoons lemon juice (optional)
about 250 ml/8 fl oz iced water	about 1 cup iced water

Sift the flour and salt onto a marble slab or other cold surface and make a well in the centre. Soften 25 g/ 1 oz/2 tablespoons butter by working with a wooden spoon (keeping the remaining butter chilled).

Put the softened butter into the well in the centre of the flour with the lemon juice (if using) and almost all the water. Work the ingredients with the fingertips until a soft elastic dough is formed, adding more water if the dough is crumbly or dry. Knead lightly, wrap in cling film or foil, then chill in the refrigerator for 15 minutes.

Sprinkle the chilled butter with a little flour or cover with greaseproof (wax) paper, then flatten it with a rolling pin to make a pliable 18 cm/6 inch square, the same consistency as the dough.

Roll out the dough on a floured cold surface to a 30 cm/12 inch square. Place the square of butter in the centre of the dough. Fold the sides of the dough over the butter, then the ends, to enclose it like a parcel. Wrap in cling film or foil, then chill in the refrigerator for 15 minutes.

Unwrap the dough and place on the floured surface, join facing downwards. Flatten it with the rolling pin, then roll it out to a rectangle three times as long as it is wide. Fold this rectangle into three by folding the top third down and the bottom third up. Seal the edges by pressing lightly with the rolling pin, keeping the edges as straight as possible.

Turn the pastry so that one of the open edges is facing towards you, then roll out into a rectangle again. Fold into three, then wrap the dough as before and chill in the refrigerator for 15 minutes.

Continue turning and rolling the dough in this way until the dough has been turned six times altogether, chilling it in the refrigerator after every two turns. After the final turn, return to the refrigerator to chill before using.

MAKES A '450 g/1 lb QUANTITY'

SOUPS

When you are served soup (potage) in France, almost without exception it will be homemade. The reason for this is very simple: in France, soup is regarded as an essential part of the meal (if not the whole part in some cases), and therefore as much care and attention goes into making the soup as it does into any other course. A perfect soup at the beginning of a meal gives a good impression of what is to follow, but remember that a soup is intended to whet the appetite, not to satiate or dull it.

The custom of eating soup in France varies enormously, not only from region to region, but also between the cities and provincial towns and rural districts. In Paris and the larger provincial towns where the main meal of the day is usually eaten in the evening, soup is served as a first course and is likely to be a clear or purée soup with a light texture. In the provinces and country districts where the main meal is more often eaten in the middle of the day, soup is served on its own in the evening, in which case it will be more substantial – a meal in itself, such as a broth with meat and vegetables.

No soup which calls for stock (bouillon or fond) will ever taste good unless it is made with a well-flavoured homemade stock, whether it be beef or veal, chicken, fish or vegetable. Recipes for stocks are given on pages 8–9, and it is well worth taking the extra time to make these yourself.
If you skimp by using a stock cube, the flavour of the finished soup will be disappointing, no matter how good the other ingredients are. Soups made with stock cubes will always have a 'samey' flavour.

French soups can be divided into three categories. Broths are simple soups made from meat or fish and vegetables in the same way as stock – the French use the same word bouillon for both broth and stock. Meat or fish and vegetables are simmered in water with herbs and seasonings for several hours, then the liquid is strained off and the meat or fish and vegetables left behind. Broths are usually more flavoursome than stocks.
In France, broths are usually poured over a thick slice of bread in the soup bowl. In some cases (as in pot-au-feu, page 68), the meat or fish from the broth is eaten afterwards as a main course.

Clear soups and consommés are made from meat and vegetables in the same way as broths, except that stock is used for the simmering liquid rather than water. After straining, the liquid is clarified with egg whites which attract all the fat and impurities. A consommé should be clear and sparkling and completely free from grease. Sometimes finely diced meat and vegetables are added.

Purée soups are made from fresh vegetables gently simmered in stock or water with flavourings and seasonings. After simmering, both vegetables and liquid are puréed until smooth. A mouli-légumes is mostly used for this purpose in France, although electric blenders and processors are now taking its place. Many purée soups are thickened – with rice, potatoes, flour or bread, for example. A soup thickened with bread is called a panade (from the French word pain meaning bread), whereas a soup thickened with cream is known as a crème. Velouté soups are thickened with flour, then enriched with a liaison of egg yolks and cream.

SOUPE À LA BIÈRE
Beer Soup

Metric/Imperial	American
25 g/1 oz butter	2 tablespoons butter
1 large onion, peeled and thinly sliced	1 large onion, peeled and thinly sliced
1 litre/1¾ pints hot well-flavoured chicken stock (page 8)	4¼ cups hot well-flavored chicken stock (page 8)
500 ml/18 fl oz light ale	2¼ cups beer
250 g/9 oz toasted fresh breadcrumbs	4½ cups toasted fresh bread crumbs
freshly grated nutmeg	freshly grated nutmeg
salt	salt
freshly ground black pepper	freshly ground black pepper
120 ml/4 fl oz double cream	½ cup heavy cream
6 slices hot toast (optional)	6 slices hot toast (optional)

Melt the butter in a pan, add the onion and fry gently for about 5 minutes. Stir in the stock and beer, then the breadcrumbs. Stir well to combine, then add nutmeg, salt and pepper to taste. Bring to the boil, then lower the heat and simmer gently for 30 minutes, stirring occasionally.

Remove from the heat, then work through the fine blade of a mouli-légumes (vegetable mill) or purée in an electric blender. Return to the rinsed-out pan, then stir in the cream and heat through very gently for a few minutes, stirring constantly. Taste and adjust the seasoning.

Pour the hot soup into a warmed soup tureen and serve immediately with slices of toast, if liked.
SERVES 6

POTAGE SAINT-GERMAIN

Split Pea Soup

Metric/Imperial	American
450 g/1 lb dried split peas	2 cups dried split peas
100 g/4 oz boned salt pork, blanched★ and cut into strips	¼ lb boneless salt pork, blanched★ and cut into strips
25 g/1 oz butter	2 tablespoons butter
1 carrot, peeled and diced	1 carrot, peeled and diced
1 onion, peeled and chopped	1 onion, peeled and chopped
2 litres/3½ pints water	4½ pints/9 cups water
1 bay leaf	1 bay leaf
1 celery stick	1 celery stalk
1 garlic clove, peeled and bruised★	1 garlic clove, peeled and bruised★
salt	salt
freshly ground black pepper	freshly ground black pepper
120 ml/4 fl oz double cream	½ cup heavy cream
croûtons, to serve (optional)	croûtons, to serve (optional)

Rinse the split peas thoroughly under cold running water, add to a pan of boiling water and boil for 5 minutes, then drain. Pat the strips of pork dry with kitchen paper towels.

Melt the butter in a large heavy pan, add the strips of pork and fry over brisk heat for 5 minutes until browned on all sides. Add the carrot and onion and continue frying for a further 2 minutes, stirring constantly.

Stir in the water and split peas, then bring to the boil. Tie the bay leaf and celery together, then add to the pan with the garlic. Add a little salt and pepper, lower the heat, cover and simmer very gently for 2 hours.

Discard the bay leaf, celery and garlic. Remove the strips of pork from the pan and reserve. Work the soup through the fine blade of a *mouli-légumes* (vegetable mill) or purée in an electric blender.

Return to the rinsed-out pan, then stir in the cream and the reserved strips of pork. Heat through very gently for a few minutes, stirring constantly. Taste and adjust seasoning.

Pour the hot soup into a warmed soup tureen and serve immediately with *croûtons* handed separately, if liked.

SERVES 6

Soupe à l'oignon gratinée; Potage Saint-Germain

SOUPE À L'OIGNON GRATINÉE

Onion Soup au Gratin

Metric/Imperial	American
100 g/4 oz butter	½ cup butter
450 g/1 lb onions, peeled and thinly sliced	1 lb onions, peeled and thinly sliced
1 litre/1¾ pints well-flavoured beef stock (page 8)	4¼ cups well-flavored beef stock (page 8)
salt	salt
freshly ground black pepper	freshly ground black pepper
12 slices French bread (baguette), toasted	12 slices French bread (baguette), toasted
150 g/5 oz Gruyère cheese★, grated	1¼ cups grated Gruyère cheese★

Melt the butter in a heavy pan. Add the onions and fry very gently for about 15 minutes or until golden, stirring frequently with a wooden spoon to prevent sticking.

Stir in the stock a little at a time, then bring to the boil. Add salt and pepper to taste, lower the heat, cover and cook gently for 30 minutes.

Taste and adjust the seasoning, then pour the soup into 4 individual heatproof soup bowls. Float 3 slices of bread in each bowl, then sprinkle over the grated cheese.

Put the bowls under a preheated hot grill (broiler) until the cheese melts and is bubbling. Serve immediately.

SERVES 4

TOURAIN TOULOUSAIN

Toulouse Egg and Cheese Soup

Metric/Imperial	American
50 g/2 oz goose fat★, dripping or butter	¼ cup goose fat★, drippings or butter
6 garlic cloves, peeled and crushed	6 garlic cloves, peeled and crushed
2 litres/3½ pints boiling chicken stock (page 8)	4½ pints/9 cups boiling chicken stock (page 8)
1 bouquet garni★	1 bouquet garni★
salt	salt
freshly ground black pepper	freshly ground black pepper
3 eggs, separated	3 eggs, separated
6 slices hot toast	6 slices hot toast
100 g/4 oz Gruyère cheese★, grated	1 cup grated Gruyère cheese★

Melt the fat in a heavy pan (preferably earthenware). Add the garlic and fry gently for 3 minutes. Add the boiling stock, bouquet garni, and salt and pepper to taste, and boil for 30 minutes.

Meanwhile, beat the egg whites lightly with a fork to break them up; do not let them become too frothy. In a separate bowl, beat the yolks together in the same way.

Whisk the egg whites into the soup with a balloon whisk. Stir a little of the hot soup into the yolks, whisking vigorously until thoroughly incorporated.

Simmer the soup for 3 minutes, then remove from the heat and discard the bouquet garni. Gradually add the egg yolk mixture, whisking vigorously all the time.

Put the slices of toast in the bottom of a warmed soup tureen, then sprinkle over the grated cheese. Pour over the hot soup and serve immediately.
SERVES 6

TOUR À LA TOMATE

Tomato and Onion Soup

Metric/Imperial	American
1 tablespoon goose fat★, dripping or butter	1 tablespoon goose fat★, drippings or butter
225 g/8 oz onions, peeled and thinly sliced	½ lb onions, peeled and thinly sliced
1 garlic clove, peeled and crushed	1 garlic clove, peeled and crushed
450 g/1 lb ripe tomatoes, quartered	1 lb ripe tomatoes, quartered
1 litre/1¾ pints chicken stock (page 8) or water	4¼ cups chicken stock (page 8) or water
1 teaspoon sugar	1 teaspoon sugar
salt	salt
freshly ground black pepper	freshly ground black pepper
2 tablespoons broken vermicelli	2 tablespoons broken vermicelli

Melt the fat in a heavy pan, add the onions and garlic and fry gently for 5 minutes until golden. Add the tomatoes, stock or water and sugar, with salt and pepper to taste. Bring to the boil, stirring, then lower the heat and simmer, uncovered, for 20 minutes.

Work the soup through the medium blade of a *mouli-légumes* (vegetable mill). Alternatively, purée in an electric blender, then work through a fine sieve (strainer).

Return the soup to the rinsed-out pan and bring to the boil again. Add the vermicelli and cook for 10 minutes until *al dente* (tender yet firm to the bite). Taste and adjust seasoning.

Pour the hot soup into a warmed soup tureen and serve immediately.
SERVES 4

The traditional *tourin* from the Aquitaine region of south-western France is French onion soup with a difference. Onions and garlic are cooked in goose fat, then simmered gently in stock and thickened with eggs.

Cheese is not usually included in a traditional *tourin*, but the soup is always poured over slices of bread in individual soup bowls – known in France as '*tremper la soupe*' or 'to soak the soup'.

SOUPE FROIDE À LA TOMATE

Chilled Tomato Soup

Metric/Imperial	American
2 tablespoons olive oil	2 tablespoons olive oil
2 onions, peeled and chopped	2 onions, peeled and chopped
2 garlic cloves, peeled and crushed	2 garlic cloves, peeled and crushed
1 kg/2 lb ripe tomatoes, quartered	2 lb ripe tomatoes, quartered
1 bay leaf	1 bay leaf
1 thyme sprig	1 thyme sprig
1 teaspoon sugar	1 teaspoon sugar
salt	salt
freshly ground black pepper	freshly ground black pepper

Potage au cresson; Soupe froide à la tomate

Heat the oil in a heavy pan, add the onions and garlic and fry gently for 5 minutes until soft. Add the tomatoes, bay leaf, thyme, sugar, and salt and pepper to taste. Cook over moderate heat, uncovered, for 25 minutes.

Discard the bay leaf and thyme, then work the soup through the medium blade of a *mouli-légumes* (vegetable mill). Alternatively, purée in an electric blender, then work through a fine sieve (strainer).

Leave until cool, then chill in the refrigerator for at least 3 hours. Taste and adjust seasoning. Serve in a chilled soup tureen.
SERVES 4

POTAGE AU CRESSON

Cream of Watercress Soup

Metric/Imperial	American
50 g/2 oz butter	$\frac{1}{4}$ cup butter
2 leeks (white part only), roughly chopped	2 leeks (white part only), roughly chopped
1 bunch watercress, leaves and stalks separated	1 bunch watercress, leaves and stalks separated
2 litres/3½ pints chicken stock (page 8)	4½ pints/9 cups chicken stock (page 8)
225 g/8 oz potatoes, peeled and diced	1⅓ cups peeled and diced potatoes
salt	salt
freshly ground black pepper	freshly ground black pepper
120 ml/4 fl oz double cream	½ cup heavy cream
croûtons fried in butter (optional)	croûtons fried in butter (optional)

Melt half the butter in a heavy pan, add the leeks and watercress stalks and fry gently for 5 minutes.

Add the stock and potatoes, and salt and pepper to taste, then bring to the boil. Lower the heat and simmer for 45 minutes, stirring occasionally.

Work the soup through the fine blade of a *mouli-légumes* (vegetable mill) or purée in an electric blender. Return to the rinsed-out pan and reheat gently.

Chop the watercress leaves. Melt the remaining butter in a separate pan, add the watercress leaves and cook gently for a few minutes. Add to the soup with the cream and bring to the boil, stirring constantly. Taste and adjust seasoning.

Pour the hot soup into a warmed soup tureen. Serve immediately with *croûtons*, if liked.
SERVES 6

Soupe aux poissons de
Marseille; Potage Crécy

POTAGE CRÉCY
Cream of Carrot Soup

Metric/Imperial	American
50 g/2 oz butter	$\frac{1}{4}$ cup butter
2 onions, peeled and thinly sliced	2 onions, peeled and thinly sliced
2 litres/3½ pints chicken stock (page 8)	4½ pints/9 cups chicken stock (page 8)
1 kg/2 lb small young carrots, peeled and sliced into thin rounds	2 lb small young carrots, peeled and sliced into thin rounds
salt	salt
freshly ground black pepper	freshly ground black pepper
3 tablespoons long-grain rice	3 tablespoons long-grain rice
120 ml/4 fl oz double cream	½ cup heavy cream

Melt half the butter in a heavy pan, add the onions and fry gently for 5 minutes until soft. Add the stock and carrots and bring to the boil. Lower the heat, add salt and pepper to taste, then simmer for 1½ hours.

Stir in the rice and simmer for a further 30 minutes or until the rice is tender. Work the soup through the medium blade of a *mouli-légumes* (vegetable mill) or purée in an electric blender.

Return the soup to the rinsed-out pan, add the cream and the remaining butter and reheat gently, stirring constantly. Taste and adjust seasoning.

Pour the hot soup into a warmed soup tureen and serve immediately.

SERVES 6

Note: 450 g/1 lb peeled and diced potatoes can be used instead of the rice.

CONSOMMÉ

Beef Consommé

Many cooks are hesitant about making their own consommé, but it is quite simple to make provided the basic stock is completely free of grease from the start. All pans and utensils should be scrupulously clean. Consommé can be served plain as in this recipe, or garnished with finely shredded beef or vegetables. Chicken and game consommé are made in exactly the same way as below, using chicken or game stock instead of beef.

Metric/Imperial	American
1.5 litres/2½ pints well-flavoured beef stock (page 8)	6¼ cups well-flavored beef stock (page 8)
450 g/1 lb shin of beef, finely shredded	1 lb shin of beef, finely shredded
1 onion, peeled and finely chopped	1 onion, peeled and finely chopped
1 carrot, peeled and finely chopped	1 carrot, peeled and finely chopped
2 egg whites, with crushed shells	2 egg whites, with crushed shells
4–6 tablespoons Madeira, port or dry sherry, to taste	4–6 tablespoons Madeira, port or dry sherry, to taste
salt	salt
freshly ground black pepper	freshly ground black pepper

Pour the cold stock into a clean enamel saucepan, then add the beef and vegetables. Whisk the egg whites to a light froth, then add to the pan with the crushed shells.

Bring the stock slowly to the boil, whisking constantly with a wire whisk. As the stock reaches boiling point, a thick white froth will form on the surface of the stock. Remove the pan from the heat immediately at this point to allow the froth to settle, then return to the lowest possible heat and simmer very gently for 40 minutes. Do not whisk or stir throughout this stage – the froth should remain completely undisturbed or the finished consommé will be cloudy.

Pour the stock carefully through a scalded cloth into a clean bowl, holding the froth back at first, then letting it slide onto the cloth at the end. Pour the stock again through the cloth to 'filter' it for the second time.

Reheat the consommé gently with Madeira, port or sherry to taste; do not allow to boil. Taste and adjust seasoning. Serve hot.

SERVES 4

Any French dish with the word *crécy* in its title will always have carrots as an ingredient or garnish. There are conflicting views on why this should be so. The town of Crécy in Seine-et-Maine does produce high quality carrots, but its best known association is with the Battle of Crécy, fought on the Somme in 1346.

SOUPE AUX POISSONS DE MARSEILLE

Marseille Fish Soup

The rock fish normally used in this recipe are commonplace in the Mediterranean. If they are impossible to obtain at your local fish market use whatever fresh fish is available to you. John Dory, red mullet, whiting, brill, sea bass and conger eel are all perfectly acceptable substitutes. Rouille, grated Parmesan and toasted baguette are traditionally served with this soup. Each slice of toast is spread with rouille, then sprinkled with Parmesan and placed in the soup before eating.

Metric/Imperial	American
7 tablespoons oil	7 tablespoons oil
2 onions, peeled and thinly sliced	2 onions, peeled and thinly sliced
2 leeks (white part only), thinly sliced	2 leeks (white part only), thinly sliced
3 tomatoes, quartered and seeded	3 tomatoes, quartered and seeded
salt	salt
freshly ground black pepper	freshly ground black pepper
6 garlic cloves, peeled and crushed	6 garlic cloves, peeled and crushed
pinch of powdered saffron	pinch of powdered saffron
3 parsley sprigs	3 parsley sprigs
1 fennel sprig	1 fennel sprig
1 thyme sprig	1 thyme sprig
1 bay leaf	1 bay leaf
1 strip fresh or dried orange peel (optional)	1 strip fresh or dried orange peel (optional)
1.5 kg/3 lb mixed fresh fish (see above), scaled, gutted and cleaned	3 lb mixed fresh fish (see above), scaled, gutted and cleaned
2 litres/3½ pints boiling water	4½ pints/9 cups boiling water
TO SERVE (optional):	TO SERVE (optional):
rouille (page 13)	rouille (page 13)
12 slices baguette, or other French bread, toasted	12 slices baguette or other French bread, toasted
50 g/2 oz Parmesan cheese, freshly grated	½ cup freshly grated Parmesan cheese

Heat the oil in a large flameproof casserole, add the onions and leeks and fry gently until soft. Add the tomatoes and fry for a further 6 to 8 minutes, stirring and pressing constantly with a wooden spoon to reduce them to a purée. Add salt and pepper to taste.

Stir in the garlic, saffron, herbs and orange peel, if using, then add the prepared whole fish. Stir well, then cover and cook over moderate heat for 10 minutes or until the fish begin to disintegrate. Pour in the boiling water and stir well. Boil rapidly for 15 minutes until the liquid has reduced by one quarter.

Pass the soup through a fine sieve (strainer), pressing firmly to work through as much of the flesh from the fish as possible, leaving behind only the bones.

Return the puréed soup to the rinsed-out casserole and reheat. Taste and adjust seasoning. Serve hot, with the *rouille*, toast and cheese handed separately, if liked.

SERVES 6

HORS D'OEUVRE & SALADS

The French term hors d'oeuvre often causes confusion amongst those who are not acquainted with the French style of eating. Literally translated, hors d'oeuvre means 'outside the work' and the term originated in the 18th century when it was the custom to eat certain dishes away from the dining table, before sitting down to the actual meal. The idea was to provide your guests with an appetizer or foretaste of what was to come, both to stave off hunger pains and to stimulate the gastric juices. Nowadays, of course, the hors d'oeuvre is always eaten at the table, usually as a first course or alternative to soup. Sometimes soup is served after the hors d'oeuvre, but in most French homes the hors d'oeuvre is eaten as a first course.

When serving hors d'oeuvre it is important to observe a few basic rules. The food should look attractive and colourful, to please the eye and stimulate the appetite, but at the same time it should not be too substantial. For this reason, portions should be kept small and are often better served on individual plates rather than on one large platter. Whether you decide to offer a selection of different hors d'oeuvre (hors d'oeuvre variés) or simply one, is a matter of personal choice. For an everyday meal in France, for example, a simple salad or a dish of vegetables tossed in a well-flavoured vinaigrette dressing is considered more than adequate as an hors d'oeuvre.

French cooks are spoilt in their choice of hors d'oeuvre by the excellence of their charcuteries. Many of the delicious salads and pâtés which you are served as hors d'oeuvre in France will have come from the local charcuterie. If you have a good local delicatessen nearby, look for Bayonne ham, cured or smoked sausages, rillettes or pâtés. Ready-made salads are expensive to buy and will always taste fresher if made at home.

If you are making up a mixed hors d'oeuvre, choose dishes which provide contrast in texture and colour, and remember to include both sweet and savoury flavours. One or two salads, together with a selection of cold cooked meats and/or pâté, hard-boiled eggs coated in a thick homemade mayonnaise, some pickled or smoked fish, and side dishes of olives or gherkins make a typical hors d'oeuvre variés.

Some of the recipes in this chapter, such as the quiches and savoury tarts, the egg and cheese dishes and the crêpes, may seem too substantial to serve as an hors d'oeuvre. These dishes were originally served as entrées, ie after the soup and the fish, but before the meat course. Although such entrées are still served on special occasions, for informal meals they are served as a first course. You will also find that many of these dishes make quite substantial lunch or supper dishes on their own or served with a salad, and many French families treat them as such.

FLAMICHE AUX POIREAUX

Leek Pie

If preferred, this pie can be made with pâte feuilletée (page 19), in which case it should be baked at 220°C/425°F/Gas Mark 7.

Metric/Imperial	American
PÂTE BRISÉE:	PÂTE BRISÉE:
250 g/9 oz plain flour	2¼ cups all-purpose flour
pinch of salt	pinch of salt
125 g/4½ oz butter	½ cup + 1 tablespoon butter
1 egg yolk	1 egg yolk
2–3 tablespoons iced water	2–3 tablespoons iced water
FILLING:	FILLING:
50 g/2 oz butter	¼ cup butter
450 g/1 lb leeks (white part only), thinly sliced	1 lb leeks (white part only), thinly sliced
pinch of freshly grated nutmeg	pinch of freshly grated nutmeg
salt	salt
freshly ground white pepper	freshly ground white pepper
3 egg yolks	3 egg yolks
120 ml/4 fl oz double cream	½ cup heavy cream
GLAZE:	GLAZE:
1 egg yolk	1 egg yolk
1 tablespoon water	1 tablespoon water

PISSALADIÈRE
Provençal Onion and Anchovy Pie

There are many versions of pissaladière, many of them with a pastry base. This version, with its base of bread dough, is not unlike the pizzas of neighbouring Italy. The name pissaladière does not come from the Italian word pizza, however, but from the French pissalat, a purée of tiny fish preserved in brine and spices which was originally used as a topping for pissaladière. If you do not have a pan or mould large enough to hold the pissaladière, it can be baked on its own on a dampened baking sheet – simply make the edges a little thicker and higher than the middle to prevent the topping spilling over during baking.

Metric/Imperial	American
DOUGH:	DOUGH:
25 g/1 oz fresh yeast	1 cake compressed yeast
4 tablespoons lukewarm water	$\frac{1}{4}$ cup lukewarm water
350 g/12 oz plain flour	3 cups all-purpose flour
pinch of salt	pinch of salt
50 g/2 oz butter, cut into small pieces	$\frac{1}{4}$ cup butter, cut into small pieces
2 eggs, beaten	2 eggs, beaten
TOPPING:	TOPPING:
6 tablespoons olive oil	6 tablespoons olive oil
1 kg/2 lb onions, peeled and thinly sliced	2 lb onions, peeled and thinly sliced
12 canned anchovies, drained and desalted★	12 canned anchovies, drained and desalted★
50 g/2 oz black olives, halved and stoned	$\frac{1}{2}$ cup halved and pitted ripe olives
freshly ground black pepper	freshly ground black pepper

Flamiche aux poireaux

Make the *pâte brisée* according to the method on page 18. Leave in a cool place for 1 hour.

Meanwhile, prepare the filling: melt the butter in a heavy pan, add the leeks and cook very gently for 30 minutes, stirring occasionally.

Remove from the heat, add the nutmeg and salt and pepper to taste, then leave to cool. Put the egg yolks and cream in a bowl and whisk together with salt and pepper to taste. Stir into the cooled leeks.

Cut off two thirds of the pastry (dough) and roll out on a floured surface. Use to line a buttered 20 to 23 cm/ 8 to 9 inch flan tin (pie pan) or flan ring placed on a buttered baking sheet.

Spread the filling in the pastry shell, then roll out the remaining pastry to make a lid and place over the filling. Moisten the edges of the pastry and pinch together to seal. If liked, decorate the top of the pie with shapes cut from the pastry trimmings, or mark the pastry with the prongs of a fork.

Beat the egg yolk and water together, then brush over the pastry lid to glaze. Bake in a preheated moderately hot oven (200°C/400°F/Gas Mark 6) for 35 to 40 minutes. Serve warm.
SERVES 6

Make the dough: dissolve the yeast in the water and set aside. Sift the flour and salt into a bowl, rub in the butter, then make a well in the centre. Add the eggs and yeast liquid, then mix together, gradually drawing in the flour from the sides of the bowl. Turn out onto a floured surface and knead well until the dough is smooth, then form into a ball and cover with a damp cloth. Leave to rise in a warm place for about 2 hours or until doubled in bulk.

Meanwhile make the topping: heat 4 tablespoons/ $\frac{1}{4}$ cup oil in a heavy pan, then add the onions. Cover and simmer very gently for about 30 minutes until the onions are soft and lightly coloured but not browned. Stir from time to time.

Knock down the dough, then knead again for a few minutes. Roll out to a circle to fit an oiled deep 25 cm/ 10 inch round baking pan or mould, then press into the pan to line the base and sides.

Spread the onions over the dough, then decorate with the anchovies and olives, making a lattice pattern if liked. Sprinkle liberally with pepper, then with the remaining oil. Leave to rise in a warm place for about 15 minutes.

Bake in a preheated hot oven (230°C/450°F/Gas Mark 8) for 30 minutes. Serve warm.
SERVES 6 TO 8

QUICHE TOURANGELLE

Touraine Quiche with Pork Rillettes

In France, rillettes can be bought at every charcuterie, although some cooks make their own (see page 30), from pork, duck, goose or rabbit. If you do not want to go to the trouble of making rillettes especially for this quiche, they can be bought in jars and cans from good delicatessens and supermarkets.

Metric/Imperial	American
PÂTE BRISÉE:	PÂTE BRISÉE:
250 g/9 oz plain flour	2¼ cups all-purpose flour
pinch of salt	pinch of salt
125 g/4½ oz butter	½ cup + 1 tablespoon butter
1 egg yolk	1 egg yolk
2–3 tablespoons iced water	2–3 tablespoons iced water
FILLING:	FILLING:
225 g/8 oz pork rillettes	½ lb pork rillettes
1 bunch fresh parsley, finely chopped	1 bunch fresh parsley, finely chopped
4 eggs	4 eggs
200 ml/⅓ pint milk	1 cup milk
120 ml/4 fl oz double cream	½ cup heavy cream
salt	salt
freshly ground black pepper	freshly ground black pepper

Make the *pâte brisée* according to the method on page 18. Leave in a cool place for 1 hour.

Roll out the pastry (dough) on a floured surface and use to line a buttered 20 to 23 cm/8 to 9 inch flan tin (pie pan) or flan ring placed on a buttered baking sheet.

Spread the pork over the pastry, then sprinkle with the parsley. Put the eggs, milk and cream in a bowl and whisk together with salt and pepper to taste. Pour into the pastry shell.

Bake in a preheated moderately hot oven (200°C/400°F/Gas Mark 6) for 35 minutes or until just set. Serve warm.

SERVES 4 TO 6

RIGHT: **Tarte à l'oignon;
Quiche Lorraine**
BELOW: **Quiche
tourangelle**

TARTE À L'OIGNON

Creamy Onion Quiche

Metric/Imperial	American
PÂTE BRISÉE:	PÂTE BRISÉE:
250 g/9 oz plain flour	2¼ cups all-purpose flour
pinch of salt	pinch of salt
125 g/4½ oz butter	½ cup + 1 tablespoon butter
1 egg yolk	1 egg yolk
2–3 tablespoons iced water	2–3 tablespoons iced water
FILLING:	FILLING:
50 g/2 oz butter	¼ cup butter
1 kg/2 lb onions, peeled and thinly sliced	2 lb onions, peeled and thinly sliced
salt	salt
freshly ground white pepper	freshly ground white pepper
200 ml/⅓ pint milk	1 cup milk
200 ml/⅓ pint double cream	1 cup heavy cream
2 eggs	2 eggs
2 egg yolks	2 egg yolks
freshly grated nutmeg (optional)	freshly grated nutmeg (optional)

Make the *pâte brisée* according to the method on page 18. Leave in a cool place for 1 hour.

Meanwhile, prepare the filling: melt the butter in a heavy pan, add the onions and cook gently for 20 minutes, stirring occasionally. Take care not to let the onions become brown; they should be soft and light golden. Add salt and pepper to taste.

Put the milk, cream, eggs and egg yolks in a bowl and whisk together with salt and pepper to taste, and nutmeg if using.

Roll out the pastry (dough) on a floured surface and use to line a buttered 20 to 23 cm/8 to 9 inch flan tin (pie pan) or flan ring placed on a buttered baking sheet. Spread the onions over the pastry base, then pour in the milk, cream and egg mixture.

Bake in a preheated moderately hot oven (200°C/400°F/Gas Mark 6) for 35 to 40 minutes or until just set. Serve warm.

SERVES 4 TO 6

TOURTE AUX ANCHOIS

Anchovy and Cheese Pie

Metric/Imperial	American
PASTRY:	PIE DOUGH:
300 g/11 oz plain flour	2¾ cups all-purpose flour
pinch of salt	pinch of salt
pinch of dried yeast	pinch of active dry yeast
7 tablespoons olive oil	7 tablespoons olive oil
about 50 ml/2 fl oz water	about ¼ cup water
FILLING:	FILLING:
225 g/8 oz Gruyère cheese★, thinly sliced	½ lb Gruyère cheese★, thinly sliced
10 canned anchovy fillets, drained and desalted★	10 canned anchovy fillets, drained and desalted★
GLAZE:	GLAZE:
1 egg yolk	1 egg yolk
1 tablespoon water or milk	1 tablespoon water or milk

QUICHE LORRAINE

Cheese is never included in the traditional quiche lorraine from the Alsace-Lorraine region of north-east France.

Metric/Imperial	American
PÂTE BRISÉE:	PÂTE BRISÉE:
250 g/9 oz plain flour	2¼ cups all-purpose flour
pinch of salt	pinch of salt
125 g/4½ oz butter	½ cup + 1 tablespoon butter
1 egg yolk	1 egg yolk
2–3 tablespoons iced water	2–3 tablespoons iced water
FILLING:	FILLING:
150 g/5 oz smoked bacon, rinds removed and cut into small pieces	5 oz smoked bacon, cut into small pieces
50 g/2 oz butter	¼ cup butter
250 ml/8 fl oz double cream	1 cup heavy cream
2 eggs	2 eggs
¼ teaspoon freshly grated nutmeg	¼ teaspoon freshly grated nutmeg
salt	salt
freshly ground white pepper	freshly ground white pepper

Make the *pâte brisée* according to the method on page 18. Leave in a cool place for 1 hour.

Meanwhile, prepare the filling: plunge the bacon pieces into a pan of boiling water for 2 minutes, then drain. Melt half the butter in a heavy pan, add the bacon pieces and cook gently until lightly coloured. Remove from the pan with a slotted spoon.

Put the cream and eggs in a bowl and whisk together with the nutmeg and salt and pepper to taste.

Roll out the pastry (dough) on a floured surface and use to line a buttered 20 to 23 cm/8 to 9 inch flan tin (pie pan) or flan ring placed on a buttered baking sheet. Sprinkle the bacon pieces over the pastry base, then dot with the remaining butter. Pour in the cream and egg mixture.

Bake in a preheated moderately hot oven (200°C/400°F/Gas Mark 6) for about 30 minutes or until just set. If the filling rises rapidly during baking, simply prick it in the centre with the point of a sharp knife. Serve warm.
SERVES 4 TO 6

Make the pastry (pie dough): sift the flour and salt into a bowl and make a well in the centre. Add the yeast and oil, then mix into the flour. Mix in just enough water to make a soft dough. Knead lightly until smooth. Leave in a cool place for 30 minutes.

Roll out half the dough on a floured surface, then use to line an oiled 20 to 23 cm/8 to 9 inch flan tin (pie pan) or flan ring placed on an oiled baking sheet. Place half the cheese in the pastry shell, cover with the anchovies, then top with the remaining cheese.

Roll out the remaining pastry and use to cover the filling. Moisten the edges of the pastry and pinch together to seal. Mix the egg yolk and water or milk together, then brush over the pastry to glaze. Bake in a preheated hot oven (220°C/425°F/Gas Mark 7) for 25 minutes until the pastry is golden. Serve warm.
SERVES 6

The French words *tarte*, *tourte* and *quiche* all mean an open, single-crust pie. Originally these were made with a base of bread dough, but nowadays they are usually made with shortcrust pastry (pie dough).

Hors d'oeuvre & Salads/29

GÂTEAU DE FOIES BLONDS DE VOLAILLE

Chicken Liver Terrine

Metric/Imperial	American
450 g/1 lb chicken livers	1 lb chicken livers
50 g/2 oz plain flour, sifted	½ cup all-purpose flour, sifted
3 whole eggs	3 whole eggs
3 egg yolks	3 egg yolks
120 ml/4 fl oz double cream	½ cup heavy cream
450 ml/¾ pint milk	2 cups milk
1 garlic clove, peeled and crushed	1 garlic clove, peeled and crushed
1–2 tablespoons chopped parsley	1–2 tablespoons chopped parsley
freshly grated nutmeg	freshly grated nutmeg
salt	salt
freshly ground black pepper	freshly ground black pepper

Work the chicken livers in an electric blender or twice through the fine blade of a *mouli-legumes* (vegetable mill). Stir in the flour, then the eggs and egg yolks one at a time.

Whip the cream until it just holds its shape, then add to the liver mixture with the milk, garlic and parsley. Add nutmeg, salt and pepper to taste, then mix well until thoroughly combined.

Pour the mixture into a well-buttered 1.2 litre/2 pt/5 cup mould and place in a hot *bain marie*. Bake in a preheated moderate oven (180°C/350°F/Gas Mark 4) for 1½ hours or until a skewer inserted into the centre comes out clean.

Leave to cool, then place a weight on top of the pâté and chill in the refrigerator overnight.

Unmould onto a serving platter and serve with hot toast.

SERVES 8 TO 10

RILLETTES DE PORC D'ANJOU

Anjou Pork Rillettes

Pork rillettes are best described as 'potted pork'. They are usually made in large quantities such as this because they keep fresh for 2 months in a refrigerator. Use equal quantities of lean and fatty pork – fillet (tenderloin), loin, belly, neck, etc.

Metric/Imperial	American
450 g/1 lb pork back fat, cut into small pieces	1 lb pork back fat, cut into small pieces
2 kg/4 lb boned pork (see above)	4 lb boneless pork (see above)
7 tablespoons water	7 tablespoons water
1 bouquet garni★	1 bouquet garni★
salt	salt
freshly ground black pepper	freshly ground black pepper
ground mixed spice	ground allspice
	ground cinnamon

Put the back fat in a heavy pan and heat very gently for about 30 minutes until melted.

Meanwhile, cut the pork into small cubes, mixing the lean and fat together. Add the pork to the pan with the water, bouquet garni and salt, pepper and spice(s) to taste.

Cover the pan and cook very gently for 4 hours, stirring occasionally. At the end of the cooking time the pork should have rendered down and become extremely soft. Any large pieces of meat can be removed at this stage with a slotted spoon and eaten separately, either hot or cold.

Pour the remaining meat and fat into small earthenware pots and leave to cool. The fat will rise to the surface of the pots and solidify, thus sealing the *rillettes*.

Cover the pots with lids, then store in the refrigerator for up to 2 months.

MAKES ABOUT 2.5 kg/5 lb

VARIATIONS

1. Add 2 to 3 cloves to the pan before cooking the pork, for added flavour.

2. For *rillettes du Mans*: use 450 g/1 lb pork back fat, 1 kg/2 lb pork and 2 kg/4 lb boned goose and make as above.

TERRINE DE LAPIN AUX PRUNEAUX

Rabbit Terrine with Prunes

Metric/Imperial	American
MARINADE:	MARINADE:
1 litre/1¾ pints dry red wine (e.g. Vouvray)	4¼ cups dry red wine (e.g. Vouvray)
2–3 tablespoons brandy	2–3 tablespoons brandy
2 tablespoons oil	2 tablespoons oil
1 carrot, peeled and finely chopped	1 carrot, peeled and finely chopped
1 onion, peeled and finely chopped	1 onion, peeled and finely chopped
1 garlic clove, peeled and finely chopped	1 garlic clove, peeled and finely chopped
6 whole cloves	6 whole cloves

Rillettes de porc d'Anjou; Terrine de lapin aux pruneaux

1 thyme sprig	1 thyme sprig
1 tarragon sprig	1 tarragon sprig
1 bay leaf	1 bay leaf
salt	salt
freshly ground black pepper	freshly ground black pepper
TERRINE:	TERRINE:
2 small rabbits (about 1.5 kg/3–3½ lb)	2 small rabbits (about 3–3½ lb)
20 prunes	20 prunes
50 g/2 oz streaky or fatty bacon, rind removed and diced	¼ cup diced fatty bacon
225 g/8 oz sausagemeat	1 cup sausagemeat
1 egg, beaten	1 egg, beaten
ground mixed spice	ground allspice
2–3 tablespoons brandy	ground cinnamon
TO FINISH:	2–3 tablespoons brandy
6 streaky bacon rashers	TO FINISH:
a few bay leaves (optional)	6 fatty bacon slices
a few thyme leaves (optional)	a few bay leaves (optional)
2 tablespoons plain flour	a few thyme leaves (optional)
	2 tablespoons all-purpose flour

Mix together the ingredients for the marinade, reserving 2 glasses wine. Cut the rabbits into small pieces, but keep the backbones intact so that the fillets can be removed whole after marinating.

Put the rabbit pieces (including the livers) in a bowl, then pour over the marinade. Cover and leave to marinate for 24 hours, turning the meat from time to time.

Put the prunes in a separate bowl and cover with the reserved 2 glasses wine. Cover and leave for 24 hours until plump.

The next day, drain the rabbit. Strain the marinade and reserve 1 glass. Remove the whole fillets from the backbones and set aside. Using a sharp pointed knife, scrape all meat from the other bones, then mince (grind) this meat with the livers.

Put the minced (ground) meat and livers in a bowl with the diced bacon, sausagemeat, beaten egg, spice(s), salt and pepper to taste and the brandy. Knead thoroughly with the hands until well mixed. Drain the prunes and remove the stones (pits).

Line a greased 2 litre/3½ pint/9 cup terrine with the bacon rashers (slices), reserving 2 rashers for the top. Press a layer of the minced meat mixture in the bottom of the terrine, arrange a few whole fillets on top, then a few prunes. Repeat these layers until all the ingredients are used up, finishing with a layer of the minced meat mixture.

Prick the top of the terrine with a skewer or fork, then slowly pour over the reserved marinade. Cover the top of the terrine with the reserved bacon rashers, pressing bay and thyme leaves in between them if liked.

Cover the terrine with a lid, then seal around the edge of the lid with a paste made from the flour and a few drops of water. Bake in a hot *bain marie* in a preheated moderate oven (180°C/350°F/Gas Mark 4) for 2 hours.

Break the pastry seal, remove the lid and leave the terrine to cool for a few minutes. Cover with a board or plate, then place heavy weights on top. Leave until completely cold, then chill in the refrigerator for 24 hours before serving.

SERVES 8 TO 10

MATAFAM
Savoury Thick Crêpe

The name matafam is derived from the Spanish, meaning literally 'to deaden hunger'. It is such a filling dish that it is quite easy to see how it came by its name.

Metric/Imperial	American
100 g/4 oz plain flour	*1 cup all-purpose flour*
200 ml/⅓ pint milk	*1 cup milk*
4 eggs, beaten	*4 eggs, beaten*
2 shallots, peeled and finely chopped	*2 scallions, peeled and finely chopped*
salt	*salt*
freshly ground white pepper	*freshly ground white pepper*
100 g/4 oz butter	*½ cup butter*

Sift the flour into a bowl, then stir in the milk a little at a time. Add the eggs and shallots (scallions), and salt and pepper to taste. Stir well until thoroughly incorporated, then leave to stand for 25 minutes.

Melt half the butter in a shallow flameproof baking dish, then pour in the crêpe mixture – it should be about 2 cm/¾ inch thick. Fry until set and golden on the underside, shaking the dish constantly to prevent the mixture from sticking.

Slide the crêpe out of the dish onto a plate, then melt the remaining butter in the dish. Invert the crêpe into the dish, cooked side uppermost, then transfer to a preheated moderate oven (180°C/350°F/Gas Mark 4) and bake for about 12 minutes. Serve immediately.
SERVES 4

VARIATIONS:
1. Add 100 g/4 oz/1 cup grated *Gruyère* cheese to the mixture with the eggs. Freshly grated nutmeg can also be added if liked.
2. In Savoie, 225 g/8oz/ 2 cups grated raw potato and strips of bacon or ham are added to the mixture with the eggs.

OMELETTE AUX CÈPES
Cèpe Omelette

If cèpes are difficult to obtain, replace with field mushrooms or button mushrooms.

Metric/Imperial	American
50 g/2 oz goose fat★, dripping or butter	*¼ cup goose fat★, drippings or butter*
450 g/1 lb cèpe mushrooms★, thinly sliced	*1 lb cèpe mushrooms★, thinly sliced*
salt	*salt*
freshly ground black pepper	*freshly ground black pepper*
2 garlic cloves, peeled and crushed	*2 garlic cloves, peeled and crushed*
1 small bunch parsley, finely chopped	*1 small bunch parsley, finely chopped*
8 eggs	*8 eggs*
40 g/1½ oz butter	*3 tablespoons butter*

Melt the fat in a heavy pan, add the mushrooms and fry until light golden in colour. Lower the heat, cover the pan and cook gently for 30 minutes if using cèpes; 5 to 10 minutes for field or button mushrooms.

Add salt and pepper to taste, then the garlic and parsley. Cover again and cook gently for a further minute.

Whisk the eggs together lightly, adding salt and pepper to taste. Add the mushrooms, reserving a few for garnish. Melt 25 g/1 oz/2 tablespoons butter in a large omelette pan, increase the heat, then pour in the egg mixture, tilting the pan to spread it evenly. Push the cooked mixture into the centre with a spatula so that the unset egg can run onto the bottom of the pan. Cook only until the underneath is set – the top of the omelette should still be soft.

Slide the omelette onto a warmed serving platter and quickly fold one half over the other. Melt the remaining butter, brush over the omelette and sprinkle with the reserved mushrooms. Serve immediately.
SERVES 4

ESCARGOTS À LA BOURGUIGNONNE
Snails with Garlic and Parsley Butter from Bourgogne

Fresh snails are time-consuming to prepare and less easily obtainable in this country than in France. If you prefer to use canned ones, omit the cleansing and boiling in the court-bouillon, and simply follow the stuffing and baking instructions.

Metric/Imperial	American
4 dozen snails	*4 dozen snails*
FOR CLEANSING:	FOR CLEANSING:
3 tablespoons coarse sea salt	*3 tablespoons coarse sea salt*
about 200 ml/⅓ pint vinegar	*about 1 cup vinegar*
pinch of plain flour	*pinch of all-purpose flour*
soda crystals	*soda crystals*
COURT-BOUILLON:	COURT-BOUILLON:
500 ml/18 fl oz dry white wine	*2¼ cups dry white wine*
500 ml/18 fl oz water	*2¼ cups water*
1 carrot, peeled and chopped	*1 carrot, peeled and chopped*
1 onion, peeled and chopped	*1 onion, peeled and chopped*
1 shallot, peeled and chopped	*1 scallion, peeled and chopped*
1 bouquet garni★	*1 bouquet garni★*
salt	*salt*
5 peppercorns	*5 peppercorns*
SNAIL BUTTER:	SNAIL BUTTER:
400 g/14 oz unsalted butter	*1¾ cups sweet butter*
2 garlic cloves, peeled and crushed	*2 garlic cloves, peeled and crushed*
20 g/¾ oz parsley, finely chopped	*1 cup finely chopped parsley*
salt	*salt*
freshly ground black pepper	*freshly ground black pepper*

Escargots à la bourguignonne; Omelette aux cèpes

Put the fresh snails in a bowl and cover with the salt, vinegar and flour. Leave for 2 hours.

Rinse the snails thoroughly under cold running water, then plunge into a pan of boiling water for 5 minutes. Drain, rinse under cold running water, then remove the shells, discarding the black intestines.

To make the *court-bouillon*: put all the ingredients, except the peppercorns, in a large pan. Add the snails, then bring to the boil. Skim off the scum with a skimmer or slotted spoon, then lower the heat and simmer very gently for 3 to 4 hours.

Add the peppercorns, simmer for a further 5 minutes, then remove the pan from the heat. Leave the snails to cool in the *court-bouillon*.

Meanwhile, wash the empty snail shells under cold running water, plunge them into a pan of boiling water to which a handful of soda crystals has been added, then boil for 30 minutes. Drain and wash the snail shells again under cold running water, then leave to dry in a sieve (strainer).

To make the snail butter: put the butter in a bowl and beat with a wooden spoon to soften. Add the garlic and parsley and beat together until creamy. Season with salt and pepper to taste.

Replace the snails in their shells, then fill each shell with the prepared snail butter. Place the snails in a special snail dish or a shallow baking dish, open ends uppermost to prevent the butter spilling out when hot. Bake in a preheated moderately hot oven (200°C/400°F/Gas Mark 6) for a few minutes, just until the butter begins to melt. Serve immediately, taking great care not to spill the butter when removing the snails from the baking dish.

SERVES 6 TO 8

VARIATIONS:
1. Substitute a little finely chopped shallot (scallion) for half the garlic in the snail butter.
2. Add a few breadcrumbs to the snail butter, with a drop or two of brandy.

The most highly prized snails to come from France are those from the vineyards of Burgundy (Bourgogne), called *helix pomatia*. These are the largest of all the snails, fattened in special snail farms on local vine leaves. They are almost always served stuffed with the classic garlic and parsley butter – known as *beurre à la bourguignonne* – from the region where snails are most bountiful.

BETTERAVES ROUGES

Beetroot (Beets) with Salt Pork

Metric/Imperial	American
100 g/4 oz salt pork, diced	½ cup diced salt pork
2 large onions, peeled and chopped	2 large onions, peeled and chopped
1 teaspoon plain flour	1 teaspoon all-purpose flour
7 tablespoons chicken stock (page 8)	7 tablespoons chicken stock (page 8)
450 g/1 lb cooked beetroot, skinned and chopped into large pieces	1 lb cooked beets, skinned and chopped into large pieces
TO FINISH:	TO FINISH:
dash of vinegar	dash of vinegar
1 tablespoon chopped herbs (e.g. chives and parsley)	1 tablespoon chopped herbs (e.g. chives and parsley)

Put the pork in a heavy pan and cook over moderate heat until the fat runs. Add the onions and fry until soft but not coloured.

Sprinkle in the flour, cook for 3 minutes, stirring constantly, then stir in the stock. Cook gently for about 10 minutes, then add the beetroot (beets). Simmer for a few minutes, then remove from the heat and sprinkle with the vinegar and chopped herbs. Serve immediately.

SERVES 4

A certain mystique surrounds soufflés, yet there are no special secrets to making them. Basically, a hot savoury soufflé is a sauce (usually béchamel), enriched with egg yolks, then lightened with egg whites and baked in the oven.

The sauce which forms the base of the soufflé should have a soft dropping consistency. If the sauce is too thin it will not hold the egg whites, if too thick, the finished soufflé will not rise properly.

The egg whites should be whisked to a volume twice that of the basic sauce mixture. For maximum volume, French chefs always use at least one more egg white than yolks, and a copper bowl and wire balloon whisk.

Adding the egg whites is possibly the most tricky part of soufflé making. The whites should be folded in with a large metal spoon, quickly, yet gently, to ensure that air is not lost from the mixture. Bake and serve immediately – a hot soufflé waits for no-one!

SOUFFLÉ AU FROMAGE

Cheese Soufflé

Metric/Imperial	American
50 g/2 oz butter	¼ cup butter
25 g/1 oz plain flour	¼ cup all-purpose flour
250 ml/8 fl oz milk	1 cup milk
2 tablespoons cream (optional)	2 tablespoons cream (optional)
4 egg yolks	4 egg yolks
150 g/5 oz Gruyère cheese★, grated	1¼ cups grated Gruyère cheese★
salt	salt
freshly ground white pepper	freshly ground white pepper
freshly grated nutmeg	freshly grated nutmeg
5 egg whites	5 egg whites

Make a béchamel sauce with the butter, flour and milk according to the method on page 44. Cook very gently for 15 minutes, stirring constantly with a wooden spoon. Remove from the heat and stir in the cream, if using.

Stir the egg yolks into the béchamel sauce one at a time, then add the cheese and salt, pepper and nutmeg to taste. Beat well, then leave to cool slightly. Whisk the egg whites until stiff, then fold gently into the sauce mixture.

Transfer the mixture to a well-buttered 1.2 litre/ 2 pint/5 cup soufflé dish, then bake in a preheated moderate oven (180°C/350°F/Gas Mark 4) for 15 minutes. Increase the heat to moderately hot (200°C/400°F/Gas Mark 6) and bake for a further 15 to 20 minutes until the soufflé is well-risen and golden. Serve immediately.

SERVES 4

SALADE DE MOULES AUX HARICOTS BLANCS

Mussel and Bean Salad

Metric/Imperial	American
3 litres/5½ pints fresh mussels	6½ pints/13 cups fresh mussels
150 ml/¼ pint dry white wine	⅔ cup dry white wine
1 clove garlic, crushed	1 clove garlic, crushed
3 tablespoons double cream	3 tablespoons heavy cream
3 tablespoons oil	3 tablespoons oil
1 tablespoon vinegar	1 tablespoon vinegar
freshly ground black pepper	freshly ground black pepper
225 g/8 oz cooked dried white haricot beans	½ lb cooked navy beans
salt	salt
2 tomatoes, sliced, to garnish	2 tomatoes, sliced, for garnish

Scrub the mussel shells clean and discard any that are open. Place in a large pan with the wine and garlic. Cover and cook over high heat for 5 to 7 minutes, until the shells open; discard any that do not. Drain and discard the mussel shells.

Put the cream in a bowl with the oil and vinegar. Add pepper to taste, then whisk with a fork until thick.

Put the beans and mussels in a deep serving dish, pour over the sauce and mix well. Season with salt to taste. Garnish with the tomato slices to serve.

SERVES 5 TO 6

SAUCISSON CHAUD, POMMES À L'HUILE

Hot Sausage and Potato Salad

This is a simple dish of spicy sausage surrounded with a hot potato salad. It is usually served as an hors d'oeuvre in France, but can equally well be served as a lunch dish. If you like the flavour of shallots (scallions), add about four of these, finely chopped, to the wine and vinegar dressing.

Metric/Imperial	American
1 kg/2 lb waxy potatoes	2 lb waxy potatoes
salt	salt
1 × 750 g/1½ lb French cooking sausage★	1 × 1½ lb French cooking sausage★
7 tablespoons dry white wine	7 tablespoons dry white wine
2 tablespoons cider vinegar	2 tablespoons cider vinegar
7 tablespoons oil	7 tablespoons oil
1 tablespoon chopped parsley	1 tablespoon chopped parsley
1 tablespoon snipped chives	1 tablespoon snipped chives
freshly ground black pepper	freshly ground black pepper

Cook the potatoes in their skins in boiling salted water for about 20 minutes until just tender.

Meanwhile, prick the sausage skin with a fork to prevent it bursting during cooking. Plunge the sausage into a pan of boiling water, lower the heat and cook gently for 20 minutes.

Drain the potatoes and remove their skins while still hot. Cut them into 1 cm/½ thick slices, then place in a heavy pan. Sprinkle over the wine, vinegar and oil, then shake the pan gently to mix the potatoes and dressing together. Place the pan over very gentle heat and reheat the potatoes.

Meanwhile, drain the sausage, leave until cool enough to handle, then remove the skin. Cut the sausage into 1 cm/½ inch thick slices and arrange in the centre of a serving platter.

When the potatoes and dressing are fairly hot, remove from the heat and sprinkle with the parsley and chives, and salt and pepper to taste. Toss gently to mix, then pile around the sausage on the platter. Serve warm.

SERVES 6

LEFT: **Soufflé au fromage**
BELOW: **Saucisson chaud, pommes à l'huile; Salade de moules aux haricots blancs**

Salade Niçoise; Salade de
poivrons grillés; Salade
verte au bresse bleu

SALADE DE POIVRONS GRILLÉS

Pepper Salad

*This is a good salad to serve with grilled (broiled) fish and
steaks.*

Metric/Imperial	American
1 kg/2 lb mixed green and red peppers	2 lb mixed green and red peppers
2 garlic cloves, peeled and finely chopped	2 garlic cloves, peeled and finely chopped
4 tablespoons olive oil	1/4 cup olive oil
1 tablespoon vinegar	1 tablespoon vinegar
salt	salt
freshly ground black pepper	freshly ground black pepper

Grill (broil) the peppers for about 10 minutes, turning
frequently, until the skin is charred on all sides.
Transfer to a bowl, cover and leave to stand for 30
minutes.

Remove the skin from the peppers, halve and
remove the seeds. Slice the flesh into thin strips.

Put the strips of pepper in a salad bowl with the
remaining ingredients, and salt and pepper to taste.
Fold gently to mix.

SERVES 4

SALADE VERTE AU BRESSE BLEU

Green Salad with Blue Cheese Dressing

Metric/Imperial	American
50 g/2 oz Bleu de Bresse cheese★	1/4 cup Bleu de Bresse cheese★
250 ml/8 fl oz double cream	1 cup heavy cream
pinch of cayenne pepper	pinch of cayenne pepper
salt	salt
freshly ground white pepper	freshly ground white pepper
2 lettuces	2 lettuces

Work the cheese and cream together until soft and well
mixed, then work through a fine sieve (strainer). Stir in
the cayenne, and salt and pepper to taste.

Separate the lettuce leaves and place in a salad bowl.
Pour over the cheese dressing and toss gently to coat
the lettuce. Serve immediately.

SERVES 5 TO 6

SALADE NIÇOISE

Niçoise Salad

*A true salade niçoise should never include vinegar in its
dressing – the juice from the tomatoes should provide enough
acid. Neither should any of the vegetables be cooked: they
should be sufficiently fresh, young and tender to be eaten
raw.*

Metric/Imperial	American
1 garlic clove, peeled and bruised★	1 garlic clove, peeled and bruised★
1 lettuce	1 lettuce
100 g/4 oz celery hearts, thinly sliced	1 cup thinly sliced celery hearts
100 g/4 oz cucumber, peeled and thinly sliced	1 cup thinly sliced peeled cucumber
225 g/8 oz small French beans, topped and tailed (optional)	1/2 lb small green beans, topped and tailed (optional)
225 g/8 oz young tender artichoke hearts, thinly sliced (optional)	1/2 lb young tender artichoke hearts, thinly sliced (optional)
450 g/1 lb tomatoes, skinned, quartered and seeded	1 lb tomatoes, skinned, quartered and seeded
1 large green pepper, cored, seeded and sliced into rings	1 large green pepper, cored, seeded and sliced into rings
1 onion, peeled and sliced into rings	1 onion, peeled and sliced into rings
4 hard-boiled eggs, halved	4 hard-cooked eggs, halved
50 g/2 oz black olives	1/2 cup ripe olives
8 canned anchovy fillets, drained and desalted★	8 canned anchovy fillets, drained and desalted★
1 × 225 g/8 oz can tuna fish in oil, drained and separated into chunks	1 × 1/2 lb can tuna fish in oil, drained and separated into chunks
DRESSING:	DRESSING:
7 tablespoons olive oil	7 tablespoons olive oil
4 basil leaves, finely chopped	4 basil leaves, finely chopped
salt	salt
freshly ground white pepper	freshly ground white pepper

Rub the inside of a large salad bowl with the bruised
garlic, then line the bowl with lettuce leaves. Chop the
remaining lettuce leaves and arrange in the bottom of
the bowl.

Mix together the celery and cucumber, with the
French (green) beans and artichoke hearts, if using.
Place in the salad bowl. Arrange the tomatoes, pepper,
onion, eggs, olives, anchovies and tuna decoratively on
top.

Mix together the ingredients for the dressing with
salt and pepper to taste. Pour over the salad just before
serving. Serve immediately.

SERVES 4

Sweet basil is a very
popular herb for
flavouring salads in
France, particularly in
Provence where the herb
grows so prolifically.
Window sills, garden
tubs and pots filled with
flourishing basil plants
are a common sight
throughout this region,
and a handful of chopped
fresh basil gives an
unmistakably
'provençal' flavour to
many savoury dishes,
apart from salads.

Tomatoes have a
special affinity with this
herb. Eggs, mushrooms
and all salad dressings
made with olive oil also
combine well with basil.

It is however one of the
stronger-tasting herbs
and should always be
used sparingly, especially
in cooked dishes, since
cooking seems to
increase its potency.

CRUDITÉS

Raw Vegetable Hors d'Oeuvre

*Crudités is a platter of prepared raw vegetables served with
a simple dressing of olive oil, vinegar and salt and pepper, or
with a variety of other sauces (see opposite), or a thick
homemade mayonnaise (page 14). Guests help themselves
to the vegetables, which are then coated in dressing or dipped
into a sauce and eaten raw. The choice of vegetables for
crudités is a personal one, governed by seasonal availability.
As long as the vegetables are young and tender, fresh and
crisp, that is all that matters.*

Metric/Imperial	**American**
6 small green peppers, cored, seeded and sliced into rings	6 small green peppers, cored, seeded and sliced into rings
1 large red pepper, cored, seeded and sliced into rings	1 large red pepper, cored, seeded and sliced into rings
1 large yellow pepper, cored, seeded and sliced into rings	1 large yellow pepper, cored, seeded and sliced into rings
1 bunch celery (white part only), separated into sticks and halved	1 bunch celery (white part only), separated into sticks and halved
2 fennel bulbs (white part only), quartered	2 fennel bulbs (white part only) quartered
8 small pickling onions, peeled	8 small button onions, peeled
2 cucumbers, thinly sliced	2 cucumbers, thinly sliced
1 bunch radishes, topped and tailed	1 bunch radishes, topped and tailed
450 g/1 lb young, tender broad beans	1 lb young, tender fava or lima beans
8 small violet-coloured artichokes, stalks, outer leaves and chokes removed	8 small violet-coloured artichokes, stalks, outer leaves and chokes removed

Arrange the prepared vegetables attractively on a large
platter or in a basket, mixing the colours as much as
possible – they look pretty arranged in the shape of a
flower. The artichokes must be immersed in a bowl of
water to which a few drops of lemon juice have been
added or they will discolour. Serve as soon as possible
after preparing the vegetables, with an oil and vinegar
dressing, thick homemade mayonnaise or the sauces
opposite.
SERVES 8

**Crudités; Anchoïade;
Tapénade; Bagna caudo**

ANCHOÏADE
Hot Anchovy Spread

Serve as a dip for crudités, or spread while still warm on slices of hot toast.

Metric/Imperial	American
12 whole anchovies in brine, drained, skinned and boned	12 whole anchovies in brine, drained, skinned and boned
500 ml/18 fl oz olive oil	2¼ cups olive oil
6 garlic cloves, peeled and crushed	6 garlic cloves, peeled and crushed
3 shallots, peeled and finely chopped	3 scallions, peeled and finely chopped
1 tablespoon red wine vinegar	1 tablespoon red wine vinegar
chopped parsley	chopped parsley
chopped thyme	chopped thyme

Rinse the anchovies thoroughly under cold running water to remove the salt. Divide them into fillets.

Crush the anchovies in a mortar, then add the oil a little at a time, as for making mayonnaise, working it into the anchovies with the pestle. Work in the garlic and shallots (scallions). Alternatively the ingredients can be worked in an electric blender.

Transfer the paste to a heatproof bowl, then stand in a hot *bain-marie* until warm, stirring constantly. Stir in the vinegar, and parsley and thyme to taste. Serve warm.

6 SERVINGS

VARIATION: Use 225 g/8 oz canned anchovies in oil instead of the anchovies in brine. Drain and desalt★ them, then mix as above with 1 garlic clove, peeled and crushed, 1 onion, peeled and finely chopped, 6 chopped basil leaves and 500 ml/18 fl oz/2¼ cups olive oil.

BAGNA CAUDO
Hot Sauce with Anchovies

Serve hot as a dip with small croutôns or crudités.

Metric/Imperial	American
15 whole anchovies in brine, drained, skinned and boned	15 whole anchovies in brine, drained, skinned and boned
75 g/3 oz butter	⅓ cup butter
3 tablespoons olive oil	3 tablespoons olive oil
5 garlic cloves, peeled and quartered	5 garlic cloves, peeled and quartered

Rinse the anchovies thoroughly under cold running water to remove salt. Divide into fillets, then slice thinly.

Melt the butter in a heavy pan, add the oil, anchovies and garlic. Heat gently, pressing the anchovies and garlic with the back of a wooden spoon until a smooth paste is formed. Serve hot.

6 SERVINGS

VARIATION: Pound the anchovies, oil and garlic to a paste with a mortar and pestle, then transfer to a heavy pan and heat through gently with half the above quantity of butter.

TAPÉNADE
Olive, Anchovy and Caper Sauce

Tapénade can be served as a dip for crudités, or it can be spread on bread. It can also be used as a stuffing for halved hard-boiled (-cooked) eggs, mixed with the mashed yolks.

Metric/Imperial	American
200 g/7 oz stoned black olives	1⅓ cups pitted ripe olives
100 g/4 oz canned anchovy fillets, drained and desalted★	¼ lb canned anchovy fillets, drained and desalted★
2 tablespoons capers	2 tablespoons capers
2 tablespoons brandy	2 tablespoons brandy
½ teaspoon prepared mustard	½ teaspoon prepared mustard
freshly ground black pepper	freshly ground black pepper
7 tablespoons olive oil	7 tablespoons olive oil

Work all the ingredients, except the oil, in an electric blender or pound with a mortar and pestle. Add the oil a little at a time, as when making mayonnaise, until a thick paste is formed. Taste and adjust seasoning, then transfer to a serving bowl.

6 SERVINGS

Provence has a style of cuisine all of its own, more Mediterranean in character than that of the other French regions and not dissimilar from the cooking of neighbouring Liguria on the Italian Mediterranean coast.

Olive trees grow all along this coastline and black and green olives are used in many dishes. Green olives are also pressed into thick, fruity olive oil, used for cooking in preference to butter, and an essential ingredient of all local salads and salad dressings.

Freshly picked, sun-ripened vegetables – tomatoes, onions, peppers, artichokes, courgettes (zucchini) and aubergines (eggplant) – are also a dominant feature of Provençal cuisine, and the locally grown garlic lends its pungent aroma and flavour to almost every savoury dish. Fresh herbs (predominantly basil) are used in abundance. Strong salty anchovies are also popular and help to give the Provençal cuisine a truly Mediterranean flavour.

Hors d'oeuvre & Salads/39

FISH & SHELLFISH

Not surprisingly, fish plays an important part in the cuisine of France, bordered as it is by the Atlantic and the Mediterranean. The vast network of rivers and streams provide an additional supply of freshwater fish.

Some of France's most celebrated dishes feature fish – classics like Sole Colbert (sole with maître d'hôtel butter) and Homard à l'américaine (lobster with tomatoes, white wine and brandy) are found on menus of top international restaurants and hotels all over the world. However, the French do not always treat their fish in such a complicated manner. Most visitors to France are pleasantly surprised to find that contrary to what they might expect, fish is usually cooked and served in the simplest of manners. It is grilled (broiled) or poached rather than fried, and more often than not is served simply with melted butter and lemon. Most fish is bought fresh from the market within hours of being landed, and is eaten on the same day, long before it has a chance to lose any of its freshness.

For poaching fish, the French use a poaching liquid called court-bouillon, made from water, vegetables, herbs and seasonings. Sometimes wine is added to, or used instead of water, especially if the fish to be poached has a strong flavour such as mackerel. Shellfish too are often poached in a wine court-bouillon. Sometimes wine vinegar is used instead of wine, although in smaller quantities, for freshwater fish which tend to have a more piquant flavour than seawater fish. A fish that is described as 'au bleu' has been poached in a vinegar court-bouillon – the acid quite literally turns the skin of the fish blue.

For delicately-flavoured fish such as whiting and turbot, and for fish steaks and fillets that need to retain their whiteness during cooking, a milk and lemon juice court-bouillon is more suitable than one made with wine or wine vinegar. There is another more concentrated liquid for poaching fish known as a fumet (page 9), but this is best reserved for mildly-flavoured fish which will benefit from its extra 'fishy' flavour.

There are literally hundreds of different varieties of fish to be found in France, and the French waste none of them, from the tiniest morsels which are no more than a mouthful, to the largest and most ugly – all are turned into delectable fish dishes. Along the Mediterranean coastline, but particularly in Provence, the custom of simple grilling and poaching is broken. Here, obscure varieties of fish are used in the traditional and unique fish stews of the area. Every fishing port from the smallest village jetty to the vast quay at Marseille, has its individual way of turning locally-caught varieties of fish – such as wrasse, rascasse and gurnard and the lobster-like petite cigale – into a fish stew of some kind. Bouillabaisse (page 46) the most celebrated of these, is best described as a cross between a stew and a soup, but there are numerous different local versions. Usually these stews are served in two parts – the broth or cooking liquid being served first as a soup, then the fish eaten separately as a main course.

NORMANDIE

FILETS DE SOLE À LA NORMANDE
Sole with Mussels, Prawns (Shrimp) and Mushrooms

This recipe is a much simplified version of the original, which included oysters and crayfish amongst its ingredients.

Metric/Imperial	American
4 sole (about 300 g/11 oz each)	4 sole (about 11 oz each)
1 onion, peeled and thinly sliced	1 onion, peeled and thinly sliced
2 carrots, peeled and thinly sliced	2 carrots, peeled and thinly sliced
1 bouquet garni★	1 bouquet garni★
400 ml/14 fl oz water	1¾ cups water
300 ml/½ pint dry white wine	1¼ cups dry white wine
salt	salt
freshly ground black pepper	freshly ground black pepper
150 g/5 oz butter	⅔ cup butter
100 g/4 oz mushrooms, stalks removed	1 cup mushrooms, stalks removed
1 tablespoon lemon juice	1 tablespoon lemon juice
1.2 litres/2 pints fresh mussels	5 cups fresh mussels
4 shallots, peeled and finely chopped	4 scallions, peeled and finely chopped
100 g/4 oz uncooked prawns	1 cup uncooked shrimp
2 egg yolks	2 egg yolks
200 ml/⅓ pint double cream	1 cup heavy cream
croûtons★ fried in butter, to garnish (optional)	croûtons★ fried in butter, for garnish (optional)

Filets de sole à la normande

Skin the sole and separate into fillets, reserving the heads and bones. Put the heads and bones in a large pan with the onion, carrots, bouquet garni, water and 200 ml/⅓ pint/1 cup wine. Bring to the boil, then lower the heat, cover and simmer for 20 minutes.

Sprinkle the sole fillets with salt and pepper. Melt 25 g/1 oz/2 tablespoons butter in a flameproof casserole, add the sole fillets, then strain the fish stock over them. Cover with foil and bake in a preheated moderate oven (180°C/350°F/Gas Mark 4) for 12 to 15 minutes, until tender.

Meanwhile, place the mushrooms in a small pan with a little water, then add the lemon juice and salt to taste. Simmer gently for 10 minutes or until cooked; drain.

Scrub the mussels and discard any that are open. Put them in a pan with the shallots (scallions) and the remaining wine. Cook over high heat until the shells open, then remove the mussels from their shells. Discard any that do not open. Reserve the cooking juices. Cook the prawns (shrimp) in boiling water for 5 minutes, then drain and shell them.

Transfer the sole to a warmed serving platter, reserving the cooking juices. Surround with the mussels, prawns (shrimp) and mushrooms. Keep hot.

Strain the cooking juices from the mussels and sole into a pan and boil steadily until reduced by three quarters. Remove from the heat. Mix together the egg yolks and cream, then stir into the reduced cooking juices. Return the pan to the heat and cook very gently for 3 to 4 minutes, stirring constantly; do not allow the sauce to boil or it will separate.

Remove from the heat and whisk the remaining butter into the sauce a little at a time. Taste and adjust seasoning. Pour the sauce over the sole and garnish with *croûtons*, if liked. Serve immediately.

SERVES 6

ANGUILLES AU VERT
Eel with Herbs

If it is difficult to obtain all the fresh herbs in this recipe, simply increase the quantity of those available to make up the same total amount. Sorrel can be replaced by spinach in this way.

Metric/Imperial	American
40 g/1½ oz butter	3 tablespoons butter
1 kg/2 lb eel, skinned, boned and cut into 4 cm/1½ inch thick pieces	2 lb eel, skinned, boned and cut into 1½ inch thick slices
3 shallots, peeled and finely chopped	3 scallions, peeled and finely chopped
120 ml/4 fl oz dry white wine	½ cup dry white wine
1 bay leaf	1 bay leaf
1 thyme sprig	1 thyme sprig
100 g/4 oz sorrel, hard stalks removed, cut into thin strips	¼ lb sorrel, hard stalks removed, cut into thin strips
100 g/4 oz spinach, hard stalks removed, cut into thin strips	¼ lb spinach, hard stalks removed, cut into thin strips
10 parsley sprigs, finely chopped	10 parsley sprigs, finely chopped
6 chive stems, snipped	6 chive stems, snipped
3 chervil sprigs, finely chopped	3 chervil sprigs, finely chopped
2 sage leaves, finely chopped	2 sage leaves, finely chopped
2 mint leaves, finely chopped	2 mint leaves, finely chopped
1 tarragon sprig, finely chopped	1 tarragon sprig, finely chopped
salt	salt
freshly ground black pepper	freshly ground black pepper
120 ml/4 fl oz double cream	½ cup heavy cream
2 egg yolks	2 egg yolks

Melt the butter in a heavy frying pan (skillet), then add the eel and shallots (scallions). Cook gently for about 5 minutes until the eel is lightly coloured on all sides.

Remove the pan from the heat and drain off the butter and cooking juices. Return the pan to the heat, add the wine, bay leaf and thyme, then cover and cook gently for 5 minutes.

Discard the bay leaf and thyme, then add the sorrel, spinach, herbs, and salt and pepper to taste. Cover again and cook gently for a further 5 minutes, or until the eel is tender.

Mix together the cream and egg yolks, then pour into the pan off the heat. Stir gently with a wooden spoon to mix the cream with the cooking juices and coat the pieces of fish.

Taste and adjust the seasoning of the sauce, then transfer the pieces of fish to a warmed serving platter. Pour the sauce over the fish. Serve immediately.

SERVES 4 TO 6

SAUMON DE L'AVEN
Salmon Brittany Style

The salmon steaks look most attractive if grilled (broiled) on a hot metal grid or barbecue. Turn them a quarter-turn every 3 minutes, then the bars of the grid will leave scorch marks on the surface of the fish.

Metric/Imperial	American
4 Dublin Bay prawns, uncooked	4 Pacific prawns, uncooked
3 tablespoons oil	3 tablespoons oil
1 carrot, peeled and finely chopped	1 carrot, peeled and finely chopped
1 onion, peeled and finely chopped	1 onion, peeled and finely chopped
2–3 tablespoons brandy	2–3 tablespoons brandy
300 ml/½ pint dry white wine (e.g. Muscadet)	1¼ cups dry white wine (e.g. Muscadet)
300 ml/½ pint water	1¼ cups water
1 bouquet garni★	1 bouquet garni★
1 garlic clove, peeled and crushed	1 garlic clove, peeled and crushed
300 g/11 oz tomatoes, skinned, chopped and seeded	1½ cups skinned, chopped and seeded tomatoes
salt	salt
freshly ground black pepper	freshly ground black pepper
100 g/4 oz butter	½ cup butter
25 g/1 oz plain flour	¼ cup all-purpose flour
4 fresh salmon steaks (about 2.5 cm/1 inch thick)	4 fresh salmon steaks (about 1 inch thick)
pinch of cayenne pepper	pinch of cayenne pepper
25 g/1 oz butter, melted	2 tablespoons butter, melted
few parsley sprigs, to garnish	few parsley sprigs, for garnish

Plunge the prawns into a pan of boiling water and cook for about 8 minutes. Drain and shell them, reserving the shells.

Heat 2 tablespoons oil in a heavy pan, add the carrot and onion and fry gently for 5 minutes. Add the prawn shells and stir vigorously over high heat. Pour in the brandy, flame it, then pour in the wine and water. Add the bouquet garni, garlic, tomatoes, and salt and pepper to taste. Cover and cook for about 1 hour.

Work the mixture through a fine sieve (strainer), pressing firmly to extract as much of the juice as possible.

Melt 25 g/1 oz/2 tablespoons butter in a heavy flameproof casserole. Sprinkle in the flour and cook for 1 minute, stirring constantly. Stir in the sieved mixture a little at a time, stirring vigorously after each addition. Bring slowly to the boil, stirring constantly, then lower the heat and simmer gently until quite thick.

Brush the salmon on both sides with the remaining oil and sprinkle with salt and pepper. Grill (broil) the steaks under a preheated moderate grill (broiler) or on a barbecue for 7 to 8 minutes on each side, until tender.

Meanwhile, add the cayenne pepper to the sauce, then taste and adjust seasoning. Remove the sauce from the heat and whisk in the remaining butter a little at a time.

When the salmon is cooked, carefully remove the skin around each steak. Place the steaks on a warmed serving platter and keep hot. Reheat the prawns by tossing them in the melted butter in a small pan over moderate heat. Garnish the salmon with the parsley sprigs and prawns. Hand the sauce separately in a sauceboat. Serve immediately.
SERVES 4

RAIE À LA NORMANDE
Skate with Cream Sauce

Saumon de l'Aven; Loup en fenouil

There are two main types of skate, the most common one being raie batis. The original French for this recipe specifies raie bouclée or thornback skate, but this is the rarer of the two outside French waters. Use whatever skate is available to you, it will make little or no difference to the finished dish.

Metric/Imperial	American
1 large onion, peeled and sliced into rings	1 large onion, peeled and sliced into rings
2 litres/3½ pints water	4½ pints/9 cups water
200 ml/⅓ pint vinegar	1 cup vinegar
1 bouquet garni★	1 bouquet garni★
1 whole clove	1 whole clove
salt	salt
freshly ground black pepper	freshly ground black pepper
1 kg/2 lb skate	2 lb skate
150 ml/¼ pint double cream	⅔ cup heavy cream
1 tablespoon drained capers	1 tablespoon drained capers
1 tablespoon chopped parsley	1 tablespoon chopped parsley
1 tablespoon cider vinegar	1 tablespoon cider vinegar

Put the onion in a fish kettle or large pan with the water, vinegar, bouquet garni, clove, and salt and pepper to taste. Boil steadily for 30 minutes, then leave the *court-bouillon* to cool.

Cut the skate into serving portions, then place in the cold *court-bouillon*. Bring slowly to the boil and simmer gently for 15 to 20 minutes. Remove the skate with a slotted spoon and drain thoroughly. Remove the skin, then place the pieces of skate on a warmed serving platter and keep hot.

Heat the cream gently in a heavy pan, then add the capers, parsley, and salt and pepper to taste. Pour this sauce over the skate, then sprinkle the cider vinegar over the top. Serve immediately.
SERVES 4

LOUP EN FENOUIL
Charcoal-Grilled (-Broiled) Bass with Fennel

A summer fish dish which must be cooked outside over charcoal for an authentic flavour.

Metric/Imperial	American
1 × 1 kg/2 lb sea bass, cleaned	1 × 2 lb sea bass, cleaned
4 tablespoons olive oil	¼ cup olive oil
salt	salt
freshly ground black pepper	freshly ground black pepper
few dried fennel stalks	few dried fennel stalks
SAUCE:	SAUCE:
2 egg yolks	2 egg yolks
1 teaspoon prepared French mustard	1 teaspoon prepared French mustard
300 ml/½ pint oil	1¼ cups oil
2 tablespoons vinegar	2 tablespoons vinegar
2 gherkins, well drained and finely chopped	2 small sweet dill pickles, well drained and finely chopped
1 tablespoon drained capers, finely chopped	1 tablespoon drained capers, finely chopped
1 tablespoon chopped parsley	1 tablespoon chopped parsley
1 tablespoon snipped chives	1 tablespoon snipped chives

Sprinkle the fish with the olive oil and salt and pepper to taste, then wrap in the fennel. Place on a grid over charcoal or under a preheated moderate grill (broiler) and cook for 25 to 30 minutes, turning the fish over carefully halfway through cooking.

Meanwhile, make the sauce: put the egg yolks in a bowl with the mustard and salt and pepper to taste and mix well. Add the oil a drop at a time, as when making mayonnaise, then pour in a steady stream once the sauce begins to emulsify, whisking vigorously all the time.

When the sauce is thick, whisk in the vinegar until thoroughly incorporated, then stir in the gherkins (dill pickles), capers, herbs, and salt and pepper to taste.

Arrange the cooked fish on a warmed serving platter. Serve immediately, removing the fennel as the fish is cut into serving pieces. Hand the sauce separately in a sauceboat.
SERVES 4

TRUITES AU RIESLING

Trout with Riesling

Use a dry Riesling for this recipe, preferably from the Alsace region of northern France.

Metric/Imperial	American
75 g/3 oz butter	⅓ cup butter
150 g/5 oz mushrooms, finely chopped	1½ cups finely chopped mushrooms
salt	salt
freshly ground black pepper	freshly ground black pepper
4 trout, gutted and cleaned through the gills	4 trout, gutted and cleaned through the gills
4 shallots, peeled and finely chopped	4 scallions, peeled and finely chopped
½ bottle (about 350 ml/ 12 fl oz) Riesling	½ bottle (about 1½ cups) Riesling
120 ml/4 fl oz double cream	½ cup heavy cream

Mix 25 g/1 oz/2 tablespoons butter in a pan and add two thirds of the mushrooms and salt and pepper to taste. Stuff the trout with this mixture.

Sprinkle the shallots (scallions) and remaining mushrooms in the bottom of a well-buttered baking dish. Place the trout on top and pour over the wine. Sprinkle with salt and pepper to taste.

Cover the dish with greaseproof (waxed) paper and bake in a preheated moderately hot oven (200°C/ 400°F/Gas Mark 6) for 20 minutes. Remove the trout from the dish, then carefully remove the skin. Arrange the trout on a warmed serving platter and keep hot.

Strain the cooking juices from the trout into a small heavy pan. Boil rapidly until reduced by two thirds, then stir in the cream. Heat gently for 2 to 3 minutes, stirring constantly, then remove from the heat and whisk in the remaining butter a little at a time. Taste and adjust seasoning. Pour the sauce over the fish and serve immediately.

SERVES 4

In France, river trout are always cooked and served simply. To smother a trout in a rich complex sauce detracts from the delicate flavour of the fish.

Truite aux amandes is one of the simplest and best-loved ways of serving trout in France. But the most famous of all French trout dishes is undoubtedly *truite au bleu*, for which the fish is plunged into a vinegar *court-bouillon* straight after killing, then served with melted butter or Hollandaise sauce and parsley.

MATELOTE À L'ALSACIENNE

Alsatian Fish Stew

This fish stew is traditionally garnished with croûtons and eaten with freshly cooked noodles, although neither of these is necessary as the dish is substantial enough to be served on its own.

Metric/Imperial	American
3 carrots, peeled and chopped	3 carrots, peeled and chopped
3 leeks, chopped	3 leeks, chopped
2 onions, peeled and chopped	2 onions, peeled and chopped
2 litres/3½ pints water	4½ pints/9 cups water
1 thyme sprig	1 thyme sprig
1 bay leaf	1 bay leaf
few parsley stalks	few parsley stalks
pinch of freshly grated nutmeg	pinch of freshly grated nutmeg
salt	salt
freshly ground black pepper	freshly ground black pepper
600 ml/1 pint dry white wine	2½ cups dry white wine
2 kg/4 lb freshwater fish (e.g. eel, tench, perch, etc.), cleaned and cut into serving pieces	4 lb freshwater fish (e.g. eel, tench, perch, etc.), cleaned and cut into serving pieces
150 g/5 oz butter	⅔ cup butter
50 g/2 oz plain flour	½ cup all-purpose flour
200 ml/⅓ pint double cream	1 cup heavy cream
3 egg yolks	3 egg yolks

Put the carrots, leeks and onions in a large pan with the water, thyme, bay leaf, parsley, nutmeg, and salt and pepper to taste. Bring to the boil, then lower the heat and simmer for 1 hour.

Strain the liquid into a clean pan, add the wine and bring to the boil again. Lower the heat, add the fish and simmer gently for about 15 minutes or until the fish flakes when tested with a fork.

Remove the fish from the pan with a slotted spoon and keep hot in a warmed serving bowl. Boil the cooking liquid rapidly until reduced to about 1.2 litres/2 pints/5 cups, then strain.

Melt 75 g/3 oz/⅓ cup butter in a separate pan, sprinkle in the flour and cook, stirring constantly, for 1 minute to obtain a smooth *roux*. Add the strained liquid a little at a time, stirring vigorously after each addition. Bring slowly to the boil, stirring constantly, then lower the heat and simmer until thick, stirring frequently. Mix the cream and egg yolks together in a bowl, then stir in a little of the hot sauce. Stir this mixture back into the pan and heat gently without boiling, stirring constantly.

Remove the pan from the heat and whisk in the remaining butter a little at a time. Taste and adjust seasoning. Pour the sauce over the fish and serve immediately.

SERVES 6 TO 8

VARIATION: Sautéed small pickling (baby) onions, diced bacon and mushrooms can be added if liked.

TRUITES AUX AMANDES

Trout with Almonds

Metric/Imperial	American
4 trout (about 225 g/8 oz each), cleaned, with heads and tails left on	4 trout (about ½ lb each), cleaned, with heads and tails left on
200 ml/⅓ pint milk	1 cup milk
1 tablespoon plain flour	1 tablespoon all-purpose flour
1 tablespoon oil	1 tablespoon oil
150 g/5 oz butter	⅔ cup butter
salt	salt
freshly ground black pepper	freshly ground black pepper
100 g/4 oz blanched almonds	1 cup blanched almonds
lemon quarters, to garnish (optional)	lemon quarters, for garnish (optional)

Dip the trout in the milk, then coat in the flour. Shake to remove excess flour. Heat the oil and 100 g/4 oz/½ cup butter in a heavy frying pan (skillet). Add the trout and cook gently for 5 minutes on each side, taking care that the butter does not burn.

Remove the trout from the pan and place on a warmed serving platter. Sprinkle with salt and pepper to taste. Keep hot.

Melt the remaining butter in the rinsed-out pan. Add the almonds and cook over moderate heat for about 2 minutes, stirring constantly, until golden on all sides. Sprinkle the almonds and butter over the trout and garnish with lemon quarters, if liked. Serve immediately.

SERVES 4

ABOVE: **Truites aux amandes**
LEFT: **Matelote à l'alsacienne; Truites au Riesling**

BOUILLABAISSE
Fish Stew from Marseille

*Bouillabaisse is served in different ways along the coast of
Provence: sometimes the fish and broth are served
separately, sometimes together in the same tureen, as in this
recipe. Guests should place a few slices of hot toast in
individual soup plates, pour over enough broth to moisten
generously, then help themselves to a few pieces of fish of
their choice.*

Metric/Imperial	American
200 ml/⅓ pint olive oil	1 cup olive oil
2 onions, peeled and thinly sliced	2 onions, peeled and thinly sliced
2 leeks (white part only), sliced into thin rings	2 leeks (white part only), sliced into thin rings
3 tomatoes, skinned, crushed and seeded	3 tomatoes, skinned, crushed and seeded
4 garlic cloves, peeled and crushed	4 garlic cloves, peeled and crushed
1 fennel sprig	1 fennel sprig
1 thyme sprig	1 thyme sprig
1 bay leaf	1 bay leaf
1 sliver fresh or dried orange peel	1 sliver fresh or dried orange peel
750 g/1½ lb small shellfish (e.g. crabs, cigales)	1½ lb small shellfish (e.g. crabs, cigales)
2 litres/3½ pints boiling water	4 pints boiling water
salt	salt
freshly ground black pepper	freshly ground black pepper
2.5 kg/5 lb fish (e.g. rascasse, John Dory, weaver, angler fish, whiting, sea bass, wrasse, etc.), cleaned and cut into serving pieces	5 lb fish (e.g. rascasse, John Dory, weaver, angler fish, whiting, sea bass, wrasse, etc.), cleaned and cut into serving pieces
4 pinches of saffron powder	4 pinches of saffron powder
24 small slices hot toast, to serve	24 small slices hot toast, to serve
ROUILLE:	ROUILLE:
2 small red peppers, cored, seeded and chopped	2 small red peppers, cored, seeded and chopped
2 garlic cloves, peeled and chopped	2 garlic cloves, peeled and chopped
pinch of saffron powder	pinch of saffron powder
50 g/2 oz crustless white bread	2 slices crustless white bread
250 ml/8 fl oz olive oil	1 cup olive oil

Heat the oil in a large pan, add the onions, leeks,
tomatoes and garlic, then the fennel, thyme, bay leaf
and orange peel. Stir well and cook gently for about
10 minutes.

Add the shellfish, boiling water, and salt and pepper
to taste. Boil for 3 minutes to allow the oil and water to
amalgamate.

Add those fish that take longest to cook first (e.g.
rascasse, angler fish) and those with shorter cooking

times (e.g. John Dory, sea bass) 5 minutes later. Cook
by boiling rapidly over high heat for 12 to 15 minutes.

Meanwhile, make the *rouille*: crush the peppers and
garlic to a paste using a mortar and pestle. Add the
saffron and salt and pepper to taste. Moisten the bread
with a little of the cooking liquid from the *bouillabaisse*,
then work into the peppers and garlic until thoroughly
incorporated. Add the oil a little at a time, as when
making mayonnaise, then pour it in a thin steady
stream as the *rouille* becomes thick.

When all the fish are cooked, taste and adjust the
seasoning of the *bouillabaisse*, then stir in the saffron.
Pour into a warmed soup tureen and serve immediately with the slices of hot toast. Hand the *rouille*
separately in a sauceboat.
SERVES 6 TO 8

FILETS DE MAQUEREAU À LA FÉCAMPOISE
Mackerel Fillets with Mussels in Cider Sauce

Metric/Imperial	American
2 shallots, peeled and finely chopped	2 scallions, peeled and finely chopped
4 mackerel, filleted	4 mackerel, filleted
salt	salt
freshly ground black pepper	freshly ground black pepper
about 400 ml/14 fl oz dry cider	about 1¾ cups hard cider
1.2 litres/2 pints fresh mussels	5 cups fresh mussels
50 g/2 oz butter	¼ cup butter
25 g/1 oz plain flour	¼ cup all-purpose flour
1 tablespoon lemon juice	1 tablespoon lemon juice
1 tablespoon chopped parsley, to garnish	1 tablespoon chopped parsley, for garnish

Spread the shallots (scallions) in the bottom of a well-
buttered baking dish. Place the mackerel fillets on top
and sprinkle with salt and pepper to taste. Pour over
half the cider. Cover the dish with greaseproof (waxed)
paper and bake in a preheated moderately hot oven
(200°C/400°F/Gas Mark 6) for 10 to 15 minutes.

Meanwhile, scrub the mussels and discard any that
are open. Put them in a pan with the remaining cider
and cook over high heat until the shells open. Discard
any that do not open. Remove the mussels from their
shells, strain the cooking juices and reserve.

Remove the mackerel from the dish, reserving the
cooking liquid, and drain thoroughly. Arrange on a
warmed serving platter with the mussels and keep hot.
Strain the cooking juices.

Melt half the butter in a heavy pan, sprinkle in the
flour and cook, stirring constantly, for 1 minute to
obtain a smooth *roux*. Add the strained juices from the
mussels and mackerel a little at a time, stirring after
each addition. Bring slowly to the boil, stirring constantly, then simmer until thick, stirring frequently.
Stir in the lemon juice, then remove from the heat and
whisk in the remaining butter a little at a time. Taste
and adjust seasoning.

Pour the sauce over the mackerel and mussels and
sprinkle with parsley. Serve immediately.
SERVES 4

It is impossible to make a
truly authentic
bouillabaisse outside the
Mediterranean waters
around Marseille, for the
fish used there are
virtually unknown
outside local waters.

In making a
bouillabaisse, many
different kinds of fish are
used. *Rascasse*, unique to
this part of the
Mediterranean, is
considered essential, but
failing this some other
white fish with firm flesh
can be used. John Dory,
angler fish (monkfish)
and weaver all make
acceptable substitutes.

In contrast, small
delicate fish must also be
included, such as *wrasse*
and whiting, and a
shellfish or two
completes the selection.
In the Mediterranean,
petites cigales (tiny
lobster-like creatures) are
added, but small pieces of
lobster (*langouste*) may be
used, and even mussels,
since these are widely
available.

Apart from the choice
of fish for *bouillabaisse*,
there are other necessary
ingredients. Olive oil and
boiling water should
form the essential part of
the broth. Onions, garlic
and tomatoes are used for
flavouring; colour is
provided by saffron.

CREVETTES AU CIDRE

Shrimp(s) or Prawns in Cider

Cooking raw shrimp(s) or prawns in cider gives them more flavour. Serve them in their shells and let guests remove the shells themselves. Be sure to provide finger bowls, napkins and a bowl for the discarded shells.

Metric/Imperial	American
750 ml/1¼ pints dry cider	3 cups hard cider
2 litres/3½ pints water	4½ pints/9 cups water
pinch of salt	pinch of salt
1 teaspoon freshly ground black pepper	1 teaspoon freshly ground black pepper
1 kg/2 lb uncooked shrimps or prawns	2 lb uncooked shrimp
thinly sliced brown bread, buttered, to serve	thinly sliced brown bread, buttered, to serve

Pour the cider and water into a large pan, add the salt and pepper and bring to the boil.

Plunge the shrimp(s) or prawns into the water, bring back to the boil and boil for 5 minutes. Drain thoroughly, then arrange on a warmed serving platter. Serve immediately with brown bread and butter.
SERVES 6

MOULES MARINIÈRE

Mussels Marinière

Metric/Imperial	American
4 litres/7 pints fresh mussels	8 pints/16 cups fresh mussels
60 g/2½ oz butter	5 tablespoons butter
6 shallots, peeled and finely chopped	6 scallions, peeled and finely chopped
1 garlic clove, peeled and crushed	1 garlic clove, peeled and crushed
600 ml/1 pint dry white wine (e.g. Muscadet)	2½ cups dry white wine (e.g. Muscadet)
1 bouquet garni★	1 bouquet garni★
freshly ground black pepper	freshly ground black pepper
2 tablespoons chopped parsley	2 tablespoons chopped parsley

Scrub the mussels and discard any that are open.

Melt the butter in a large pan, add the shallots (scallions) and garlic and fry gently until soft but not coloured.

Stir in the wine, then add the bouquet garni and bring to the boil. Boil for 2 minutes, then add pepper to taste and the mussels.

Shake or stir the mussels vigorously over high heat until the shells open, then remove from the pan with a slotted spoon and set aside, discarding any that have not opened.

Boil the liquid rapidly until reduced by half, then return the mussels to the pan and heat through for 1 minute, shaking the pan constantly.

Sprinkle with the parsley, then shake the pan again. Pile the mussels in a warmed deep serving dish, discarding the bouquet garni. Serve immediately.
SERVES 6

ÉCREVISSES À LA CHAMPENOISE

Crayfish in Champagne and Cream Sauce

A recipe to reserve for very special occasions.

Metric/Imperial	American
36 crayfish	36 crayfish
50 g/2 oz butter	¼ cup butter
4 shallots, peeled and finely chopped	4 scallions, peeled and finely chopped
½ bottle champagne	½ bottle champagne
salt	salt
freshly ground black pepper	freshly ground black pepper
300 ml/½ pint double cream	1¼ cups heavy cream
pinch of cayenne pepper	pinch of cayenne pepper
2 teaspoons chopped tarragon, to garnish	2 teaspoons chopped tarragon, for garnish

Gut the crayfish by pulling the middle fin on the tail. Twist sharply to remove black thread, stomach and intestines. Wash the crayfish thoroughly under cold running water.

Melt the butter in a flameproof casserole, add the shallots (scallions) and fry gently for 5 minutes until soft but not coloured. Pour in the champagne, add salt and pepper to taste, then bring to the boil and boil for 4 minutes.

Add the crayfish, cover and cook for 10 minutes, stirring occasionally. Remove the crayfish with a slotted spoon, drain and arrange on a warmed serving platter. Keep hot.

Boil the cooking liquid rapidly until reduced by half. Stir in the cream, then cook until the sauce is thick, stirring constantly. Add the cayenne, taste and adjust seasoning, then pour through a fine sieve (strainer) over the crayfish. Sprinkle with the tarragon and serve immediately.
SERVES 6

MOUCLADE

Mussels with White Wine and Cream Sauce

A more ritzy version of the classic moules marinière.

Metric/Imperial	American
3 litres/5½ pints fresh mussels	6½ pints/13 cups fresh mussels
400 ml/14 fl oz dry white wine (e.g. Muscadet)	1¾ cups dry white wine (e.g. Muscadet)
1 bay leaf	1 bay leaf
1 thyme sprig	1 thyme sprig
3 parsley stalks, bruised	3 parsley stalks, bruised
25 g/1 oz butter	2 tablespoons butter
3 shallots, peeled and finely chopped	3 scallions, peeled and finely chopped
150 ml/¼ pint double cream	⅔ cup heavy cream
pinch of cayenne pepper	pinch of cayenne pepper
3 egg yolks	3 egg yolks
1 teaspoon curry powder	1 teaspoon curry powder

This version of *mouclade* is spiced with cayenne pepper and curry powder, which may seem unusual ingredients in French cookery. However, in the days of the slave trade, spices were brought to the French ports on the Atlantic coast. African slaves employed by the wealthy French often used these spices in cooking. Recipes like this one retain the flavour of those times.

Scrub the mussels and discard any that are open. Bring the wine to the boil in a large pan with the bay leaf, thyme and parsley. Add the mussels and shake the pan over high heat until the shells open. Remove the mussels from the pan with a slotted spoon, discarding any that have not opened, and set aside.

Continue boiling the liquid in the pan. Meanwhile, melt the butter in a separate pan, add the shallots (scallions) and fry gently for 1 to 2 minutes. Stir the wine and mussel liquid slowly into the pan (taking care not to add any sediment from the bottom), then boil rapidly until reduced by half.

Pour the reduced liquid through a fine sieve (strainer) into a clean pan. Stir in two thirds of the cream and the cayenne and bring to the boil. Boil to reduce for 1 minute.

Meanwhile, put the egg yolks in a bowl with the remaining cream and the curry powder. Whisk with a fork, then gradually whisk in 2 tablespoons of the hot liquid. Whisk this mixture slowly back into the pan over the lowest possible heat and heat through very gently, stirring constantly. Do not allow the liquid to boil or it will separate. Taste and adjust seasoning.

Add the mussels to the sauce and heat through for 1 minute, shaking the pan constantly to coat each mussel in sauce. Divide the mussels and sauce equally between 4 warmed individual serving bowls. Serve immediately.
SERVES 4 TO 6

VARIATION: Brandy can be added to the sauce for extra flavour, also crushed garlic and/or finely chopped parsley.

Crevettes au cidre; Ecrevisses à la champenoise; Moules marinière

POULTRY & GAME

Poultry is cooked and served in all manner of ways in France, from stuffing and roasting a whole bird, poaching it with vegetables and liquid, to grilling, sautéeing, and frying it in butter. From the simple methods of regional cookery to the classic dishes of la haute cuisine, the French have a way with chicken.

Not for the French housewife the deep-frozen chickens and chicken portions that are so popular in other countries; poultry is invariably brought fresh and free-range – and in country districts still with its feathers on and clucking! If chickens from the Bresse region are available then so much the better, for these are the most highly prized for quality, tenderness, succulence and flavour. Local markets throughout France are ideal places to select poussin, chicken, plump capon or freshly killed turkey. Even cockerels and old hens are not scorned in France, for the right amount of long, slow simmering in stock or wine, with herbs and seasonings, or with a succulent stuffing, turn these birds into tasty dishes. For good quality chickens, simple methods – like roasting in butter and tarragon, or sautéeing in butter then serving with a sprinkling of lemon juice and parsley – are just as popular as stuffing and roasting.

Although not so widely available as chicken, duck and geese are immensely popular in France, for their richness of flavour. Ducks from Nantes and Rouen are the most highly prized, and the region of Languedoc is famous for its geese. The whole of south-western France is dedicated to the rearing of geese, not only for their specially fattened livers, (foie gras) but also for their fat and the famous delicacy – confit d'oie or preserved goose.

Guinea fowl, pigeon, partridge and pheasant are also very popular in France, both domesticated and wild, particularly in country districts where shooting is a common pastime, for the French game laws are not so restrictive as they are in other countries. Recipes for game birds and animals are therefore prolific in France, and it is well worth experimenting with them as a welcome change from poultry.

BOURGOGNE

COQ AU VIN
Chicken in Red Wine

Metric/Imperial	American
2 tablespoons oil	2 tablespoons oil
50 g/2 oz butter	¼ cup butter
1 × 2.5 kg/5 lb chicken, cut into 12 serving pieces	1 × 5 lb chicken, cut into 12 serving pieces
24 small pickling onions, peeled	24 baby onions, peeled
100 g/4 oz smoked bacon, rind removed and diced	½ cup diced smoked bacon
1 tablespoon plain flour	1 tablespoon all-purpose flour
1 bottle good red wine (e.g. Burgundy, Champigny or Pomerol)	1 bottle good red wine (e.g. Burgundy, Champigny or Pomerol)
1 bouquet garni★	1 bouquet garni★
2 garlic cloves	2 garlic cloves
pinch of sugar	pinch of sugar
freshly grated nutmeg	freshly grated nutmeg
salt	salt
freshly ground black pepper	freshly ground black pepper
24 button mushrooms	24 button mushrooms
1 tablespoon brandy	1 tablespoon brandy
12 large croûtes★	12 large croûtes★

Coq au vin

Heat the oil and butter in a large flameproof casserole, add the chicken pieces and fry gently until golden on all sides. Remove from the casserole with a slotted spoon and set aside.

Pour off half the fat from the casserole, then add the onions and bacon. Fry over moderate heat until lightly coloured, then sprinkle in the flour and stir well.

Pour in the wine and bring to the boil, then add the bouquet garni, garlic cloves (unpeeled), sugar, and nutmeg, salt and pepper to taste. Return the chicken to the casserole, lower the heat, cover and simmer for 15 minutes.

Add the mushrooms, then continue cooking gently for a further 45 minutes or until the chicken is tender. Remove the chicken with a slotted spoon and arrange on a warmed serving platter. Keep hot.

Pour the brandy into the sauce and boil, uncovered, for 5 minutes until reduced to about 300 ml/$\frac{1}{2}$ pint/ 1$\frac{1}{4}$ cups. Remove the bouquet garni and garlic cloves. Taste and adjust seasoning.

Pour the sauce over the chicken, then surround with the *croûtes*. Serve immediately.

SERVES 6 TO 8

POULE AU POT À LA TOULOUSAINE

Stuffed Chicken with Vegetables

Ideally, this chicken casserole should be cooked over the lowest possible heat for the longest possible time – to ensure the flavour of the stock is very rich. Years ago it would be cooked in a cast iron pot over the fire and left overnight. These days it is best cooked gently on top of the stove or in the oven on a very low setting.

Metric/Imperial	American
STUFFING:	STUFFING:
150 g/5 oz fresh breadcrumbs	2$\frac{1}{2}$ cups fresh bread crumbs
225 g/8 oz fatty ham, finely chopped	1 cup finely chopped fatty ham
8 garlic cloves, peeled and crushed	8 garlic cloves, peeled and crushed
1 tablespoon chopped parsley	1 tablespoon chopped parsley
freshly grated nutmeg	freshly grated nutmeg
salt	salt
freshly ground black pepper	freshly ground black pepper
liver and gizzard from chicken, finely chopped (optional)	liver and gizzard from chicken, finely chopped (optional)
2 eggs, beaten	2 eggs, beaten
1 × 2 kg/4–4$\frac{1}{2}$ lb chicken	1 × 4–4$\frac{1}{2}$ lb chicken
3 litres/5$\frac{1}{2}$ pints water	6$\frac{1}{2}$ pints/13 cups water
3 carrots, peeled	3 carrots, peeled
2 turnips, peeled	2 turnips, peeled
4 leeks (white part only)	4 leeks (white part only)
2 onions, peeled and stuck with 5 whole cloves	2 onions, peeled and stuck with 5 whole cloves
1 bouquet garni★	1 bouquet garni★
100 g/4 oz vermicelli or 6 slices hot toast, to serve (optional)	$\frac{1}{4}$ lb vermicelli or 6 slices hot toast, to serve (optional)

Prepare the stuffing: put the breadcrumbs in a bowl with the ham, 2 garlic cloves, parsley and nutmeg, salt and pepper to taste. Stir well to mix. If liked, add the chopped liver and gizzard from the chicken. Bind with the beaten eggs.

Put the stuffing in the chicken cavity, then truss with thread or fine string. Bring the water to the boil in a large flameproof casserole with the vegetables, bouquet garni and salt and pepper to taste.

Place the chicken in the casserole, cover and cook gently for 3 to 3$\frac{1}{2}$ hours until the chicken is very tender and the stock rich with flavour.

To serve, remove the chicken from the stock and cut into serving pieces. Slice the stuffing. Keep the chicken and stuffing hot.

Discard the bouquet garni from the stock and cut the vegetables into bite-sized pieces. Reheat, adding the vermicelli if serving. Taste and adjust seasoning. Serve hot as a soup for a first course. If serving with toast rather than vermicelli, pour over slices of hot toast in individual soup bowls. Serve the chicken and stuffing separately as a main course.

SERVES 6

POULET VALLÉE D'AUGE

Chicken with Mushrooms, Cider and Cream

There are numerous recipes for poulet vallée d'auge. Madeira may be used instead of the cider, and the chicken can also be flambéed in calvados. Small pickling onions sometimes replace mushrooms. The usual accompaniments are sautéed potatoes and a julienne★ of mixed vegetables such as carrots, onions, turnips and leeks.

Metric/Imperial	American
75 g/3 oz butter	1/3 cup butter
1 × 1.5 kg/3¼–3½ lb chicken, cut into 4–6 serving pieces	1 × 3¼–3½ lb chicken, cut into 4–6 serving pieces
salt	salt
freshly ground black pepper	freshly ground black pepper
450 g/1 lb mushrooms, finely chopped	4 cups finely chopped mushrooms
200 ml/⅓ pint dry cider	1 cup hard cider
120 ml/4 fl oz double cream	½ cup heavy cream

Melt 50 g/2 oz/¼ cup butter in a large flameproof casserole, add the chicken pieces and fry gently until golden on all sides. Sprinkle with salt and pepper to taste, cover and cook gently for 10 minutes.

Melt the remaining butter in a separate pan, add the mushrooms and cook gently until their juices run into the butter. Pour off the liquid into the casserole, draining the mushrooms thoroughly. Pour in the cider, add salt and pepper to taste, then cover and simmer gently for 45 minutes or until the chicken is tender.

Remove the chicken and set aside. Stir the cream into the casserole and simmer until thick, stirring constantly. Return the chicken to the casserole, add the mushrooms and simmer for a few minutes to reheat. Taste and adjust the seasoning. Serve immediately.

SERVES 4 TO 6

POULET AU FROMAGE

Chicken with Gruyère, White Wine and Cream

Metric/Imperial	American
50 g/2 oz butter	¼ cup butter
4 chicken portions	4 chicken portions
1 shallot, peeled and finely chopped	1 scallion, peeled and finely chopped
300 ml/½ pint dry white wine	1¼ cups dry white wine
300 ml/½ pint double cream	1¼ cups heavy cream
freshly grated nutmeg	freshly grated nutmeg
salt	salt
freshly ground black pepper	freshly ground black pepper
1 tablespoon prepared French mustard	1 tablespoon prepared French mustard
100 g/4 oz Gruyère cheese★, grated	1 cup grated Gruyère cheese★

Melt 40 g/1½ oz/3 tablespoons butter in a large flameproof casserole, add the chicken and shallot (scallion) and fry over moderate heat until the chicken is lightly coloured on all sides.

Pour in the wine and cream. Add nutmeg, salt and pepper to taste, then bring to the boil. Stir in the mustard, then half of the cheese. Stir well, then cover and cook very gently for 1 hour or until the chicken is tender.

Taste and adjust the seasoning of the sauce, then transfer the chicken and sauce to a flameproof serving dish. Sprinkle with the reserved cheese and dot with the remaining butter. Put under a preheated hot grill (broiler) for a few minutes until golden brown. Serve immediately.

SERVES 4

POULET AU VERJUS

Chicken with Grapes

Verjus or verjuice was used extensively in cooking as a flavouring or condiment hundreds of years ago, but it is little used today. Originally it was the juice of a special variety of unripe grapes of the same name, preserved by evaporation which gave it a concentrated flavour. These days we have to use fresh green grapes to provide a similar, less strong flavour.

Metric/Imperial	American
2 tablespoons goose fat★ or butter	2 tablespoons goose fat★ or butter
6 small pickling onions, peeled	6 baby onions, peeled
1 × 1.5 kg/3¼–3½ lb chicken, cut into 8 serving pieces with the liver reserved and chopped	1 × 3¼–3½ lb chicken, cut into 8 serving pieces with the liver reserved and chopped
2 garlic cloves, peeled and crushed	2 garlic cloves, peeled and crushed
120 ml/4 fl oz chicken stock (page 8)	½ cup chicken stock (page 8)
salt	salt
freshly ground black pepper	freshly ground black pepper
about 225 g/8 oz ripe green grapes, skinned and seeded	about ½ cup ripe green grapes, skinned and seeded
chopped parsley	chopped parsley

Melt the fat or butter in a large flameproof casserole, add the onions and fry over moderate heat until lightly coloured. Remove with a slotted spoon, then place the chicken pieces in the casserole and fry gently until golden on all sides.

Return the onions to the casserole, then add the garlic and stock, and salt and pepper to taste. Cook gently for 30 minutes.

Add the grapes to the chicken, with the chopped liver and parsley to taste. Boil rapidly for 15 minutes to thicken the sauce. Taste and adjust seasoning, then transfer to a warmed serving dish. Serve immediately.

SERVES 4

Although frozen and chilled chickens are available in France, freshly killed birds, available at the local market, are still more popular. Maize is the favourite cereal for feeding poultry in France, and it is this which gives the birds their appetizing golden-yellow colour.

Poulets de Bresse are the most highly prized chickens throughout the whole of France; fed on maize and dairy products, their breeding is strictly controlled to 1 million birds each year, and regulations are laid down as to the number of birds reared together.

Anyone who has ever had the good fortune to eat *poulet de Bresse* will appreciate the true meaning of the term 'free-range'.

PÉRIGORD

COQ EN PÂTE

Stuffed Chicken in Pastry

*Truffles are very expensive to use in a stuffing like this,
where they may not be fully appreciated. Use button
mushrooms for a more economical stuffing. Sausagemeat can
replace the foie gras for the same reason. Alternatively,
paté de foie gras aux truffes, makes a good substitute for both.
In Périgord where truffles are prolific, this would be served
with the classic Sauce périgueux. Outside Périgord, where
they are prohibitively expensive, sauce poulette (page 13)
would make an acceptable alternative.*

Metric/Imperial	American
STUFFING:	STUFFING:
liver from chicken, finely chopped	liver from chicken, finely chopped
100 g/4 oz sausagemeat	½ cup sausagemeat
225 g/8 oz foie gras★	½ lb foie gras★
50 g/2 oz canned truffles★, drained and thinly sliced, juice reserved (optional)	2 oz canned truffles★, drained and thinly sliced, juice reserved (optional)
1 tablespoon brandy	1 tablespoon brandy
salt	salt
freshly ground black pepper	freshly ground black pepper
1 × 1.5 kg/3¼–3½ lb chicken	1 × 3¼–3½ lb chicken
50 g/2 oz butter, softened	¼ cup softened butter
400 g/14 oz pâte feuilletée (page 19)	14 oz pâte feuilletée (page 19)
1 egg yolk mixed with a little milk, to glaze	1 egg yolk mixed with a little milk, to glaze

Prepare the stuffing: put the chicken liver in a bowl
with the sausagemeat, foie gras and truffles (if using).
Mix well, add the brandy, juice from the truffles (if
using) and salt and pepper to taste. Mix well again.

Put the stuffing in the chicken cavity, then truss with
thread or fine string. Place the chicken in a roasting
pan, brush with the softened butter and sprinkle with
salt and pepper. Roast in a preheated hot oven
(220°C/425°F/Gas Mark 7) for 20 minutes, then reduce
the temperature to moderately hot (200°C/400°F/Gas
Mark 6) and cook for another 20 minutes.

Meanwhile, roll out the pastry on a floured surface
until large enough to wrap around the whole chicken.

Remove the chicken from the oven, leave until cool
enough to handle, then remove the thread or string.
Place the chicken in the centre of the pastry, then wrap
the pastry around the chicken to enclose it completely.
Moisten the edges with water and seal firmly. Make a
small hole in the top of the pastry, and decorate with
pastry trimmings, if liked.

Stand the chicken parcel on a dampened baking
sheet and brush all over with the egg yolk mixture.
Bake in the moderately hot oven for 45 minutes until
the pastry is golden brown and crisp.

To serve, remove the pastry, then cut the chicken
into serving pieces, scooping out the stuffing. Let
guests help themselves to slices of pastry, chicken and
stuffing. Serve *sauce poulette* separately in a sauceboat.
SERVES 4 TO 6

Coq en pâte; Poulet
vallée d'Auge

POULET SAUTÉ BASQUAISE

Sautéed Chicken with Peppers, Tomatoes, Ham and Sausage

In the Basque country, this dish would be garnished with the small spicy sausages known as louquenkas, which are peculiar to the region. They are not unlike the Spanish chorizos, which may be used as a substitute.

Metric/Imperial	American
2 tablespoons oil	2 tablespoons oil
50 g/2 oz butter	$\frac{1}{4}$ cup butter
1 × 1.5 kg/$3\frac{1}{4}$–$3\frac{1}{2}$ lb chicken, cut into 8 serving pieces	1 × $3\frac{1}{4}$–$3\frac{1}{2}$ lb chicken, cut into 8 serving pieces
1 onion, peeled and finely chopped	1 onion, peeled and finely chopped
2 garlic cloves, peeled and crushed	2 garlic cloves, peeled and crushed
6 green peppers, cored, seeded and thinly sliced	6 green peppers, cored, seeded and thinly sliced
4 tomatoes, skinned, chopped and seeded	4 tomatoes, skinned, chopped and seeded
salt	salt
freshly ground black pepper	freshly ground black pepper
120 ml/4 fl oz dry white wine	$\frac{1}{2}$ cup dry white wine
GARNISH:	GARNISH:
225 g/8 oz cooked ham★, diced	1 cup diced cooked ham★
6 small spicy sausages★, thickly sliced	6 small spicy sausages★, thickly sliced
chopped parsley	chopped parsley

Heat the oil and butter in a large flameproof casserole, add the chicken pieces and fry over moderate heat until lightly coloured on all sides. Remove from the casserole with a slotted spoon and set aside.

Add the onion to the casserole with the garlic, peppers, tomatoes, and salt and pepper to taste. Cook over brisk heat for about 10 minutes, stirring constantly, then pour in the wine. Bring to the boil, then lower the heat and add the chicken pieces. Cook gently for 45 minutes to 1 hour or until the chicken is tender.

Just before the end of the cooking time, put the ham and sausage in a separate pan and toss gently over moderate heat until hot, taking care not to overcook and toughen the meat.

Taste and adjust the seasoning of the sauce, then arrange the chicken and sauce in the centre of a warmed serving platter. Sprinkle with chopped parsley to taste. Alternate the ham and sausage around the edge of the platter. Serve immediately.
SERVES 4

POULET AUX QUARANTE GOUSSES D'AIL

Chicken with Forty Garlic Cloves

It is customary to serve this dish with slices of hot toast. Divide the cooked garlic cloves equally amongst your guests, who should then spread the garlic over the toast themselves. The garlic will be so soft from the long cooking, that it will mash to a purée (paste) and the garlic skins will come away easily.

Metric/Imperial	American
1 × 1.75 kg/4 lb chicken	1 × 4 lb chicken
salt	salt
1 bouquet garni★	1 bouquet garni★
40 garlic cloves	40 garlic cloves
200 ml/⅓ pint oil	1 cup oil
few rosemary, thyme, sage and parsley leaves	few rosemary, thyme, sage and parsley leaves
1 celery stick, chopped	1 celery stalk, chopped
freshly ground black pepper	freshly ground black pepper
2 tablespoons plain flour, for sealing	2 tablespoons all-purpose flour, for sealing
6 slices hot toast, to serve	6 slices hot toast, to serve

Sprinkle the inside of the chicken with salt, then place the bouquet garni in the cavity. Truss the chicken with thread or fine string.

Separate the garlic cloves, but do not peel them. Heat the oil in a large flameproof casserole, add the garlic, herbs and celery, then the chicken. Turn the chicken over to coat in the oil and herbs, then sprinkle with salt and pepper to taste.

Cover the casserole with a lid, then seal around the edge of the lid with a paste made from the flour and a few drops of water.

Bake in a preheated moderate oven (180°C/350°F/ Gas Mark 4) for 1½ hours, without opening the lid.

Break the seal and transfer the chicken and garlic to a warmed serving platter. Serve immediately, with the toast.

SERVES 6

DINDE AUX MARRONS

Turkey with Chestnut and Sausagemeat Stuffing

Metric/Imperial	American
450 g/1 lb chestnuts	1 lb chestnuts
450 g/1 lb sausagemeat	2 cups sausagemeat
1 tablespoon chopped herbs (e.g. chives, parsley, tarragon)	1 tablespoon chopped herbs (e.g. chives, parsley, tarragon)
7 tablespoons brandy	7 tablespoons brandy
freshly grated nutmeg	freshly grated nutmeg
salt	salt
freshly ground black pepper	freshly ground black pepper
1 egg, beaten	1 egg, beaten
1 × 4 kg/9 lb turkey	1 × 9 lb turkey
chestnuts to garnish (optional)	chestnuts to garnish (optional)

Plunge the chestnuts into boiling water and simmer for 10 minutes. Drain and peel, then simmer in fresh water for about 30 minutes or until tender.

Drain the chestnuts thoroughly, then crumble them roughly in a bowl. Add the sausagemeat, herbs and brandy, with nutmeg, salt and pepper to taste. Mix well until thoroughly combined, then add enough egg to bind the mixture. Mince (grind) or finely chop the liver from the turkey, then mix into the stuffing until evenly distributed.

Put the stuffing inside the cavity of the turkey, then truss with thread or fine string. Place on a rack in a roasting pan and roast in a preheated moderately hot oven (200°C/400°F/Gas Mark 6) for 15 minutes. Lower the temperature to moderate (180°C/350°F/Gas Mark 4) and cook for a further 2¼ hours or until the turkey is tender. (To test if the turkey is cooked, pierce the thickest part of the thigh with a skewer – the juices should run clear.) Baste the turkey occasionally during cooking.

Serve the turkey hot on a warmed serving platter. Surround with whole peeled chestnuts, poached until tender as for the stuffing above, if liked.

SERVES 8 TO 10

NOTE: This stuffing can also be used for goose.

Poulet sauté basquaise; Poulet aux quarante gousses d'ail

Meanwhile, heat half the calvados in a small pan, flame it, then pour over the duck. When the flames have died down, transfer the duck to a board and cut into serving pieces (legs, wings and thin slivers of breast meat). Discard the bacon and threads.

Place the duck on a plate, cover tightly, then stand the plate over a pan of hot water to keep the duck moist and hot.

Pour the cider into a heavy pan and boil vigorously until reduced by half. Stir in the cream, a little at a time, then simmer until reduced and glossy, stirring constantly. Taste and adjust seasoning.

Arrange the duck in the centre of a warmed serving platter. Remove the potatoes from the roasting pan, with a slotted spoon, then arrange around the duck. Sprinkle with the remaining calvados. Pour a little of the sauce over the duck. Serve hot, with the remaining sauce handed separately in a sauceboat.
SERVES 4 TO 6

ALSACE-LORRAINE

CANARD AUX HERBES
Duck with Herbs

If sorrel is difficult to obtain, use double the quantity of spinach. The herbs can be varied according to taste and availability. Steamed or boiled potatoes are the usual accompaniment to this dish.

Metric/Imperial	American
100 g/4 oz streaky bacon, diced	*½ cup diced fatty bacon*
1 × 2–2.5 kg/4–5 lb duck, cut into 6 serving pieces	*1 × 4–5 lb duck, cut into 6 serving pieces*
100 g/4 oz sorrel, shredded	*1½ cups shredded sorrel*
100 g/4 oz spinach, shredded	*1½ cups shredded spinach*
100 g/4 oz lettuce, shredded	*1½ cups shredded lettuce*
2 leeks (white part only), thinly sliced	*2 leeks (white part only), thinly sliced*
3 celery sticks, thinly sliced	*3 celery stalks, thinly sliced*
3 tarragon sprigs, finely chopped	*3 tarragon sprigs, finely chopped*
3 parsley sprigs, finely chopped	*3 parsley sprigs, finely chopped*
3 mint sprigs, finely chopped	*3 mint sprigs, finely chopped*
1 bunch chives, snipped	*1 bunch chives, snipped*
1 tablespoon plain flour	*1 tablespoon all-purpose flour*
200 ml/⅓ pint dry white wine	*1 cup dry white wine*
120 ml/4 fl oz double cream	*½ cup heavy cream*
salt	*salt*
freshly ground black pepper	*freshly ground black pepper*

Put the bacon in a heavy flameproof casserole and heat gently until the fat runs. Add the duck pieces and sauté for 15 to 20 minutes until well browned. Drain off all but 2 tablespoons of the fat.

Add the vegetables and herbs to the casserole, then sprinkle in the flour and cook, stirring for 1 minute. Add the wine and cream, then continue cooking gently for a further 30 minutes or until the duck is tender. Add salt and pepper to taste. Serve hot.
SERVES 6

Cider, cream and calvados, the three ingredients for which Normandy is famous, are all included in this recipe for *bonhomme normand*. What Normandy lacks in the way of vineyards, it more than compensates for in prolific orchards.

Cider and calvados are both produced from local apples, and apples are used extensively in the regional cooking of Normandy. Cider, combined with local butter and cream, makes wonderfully rich sauces to complement pork, veal and chicken, as well as the duck dishes of the region.

Calvados, unique to this region, is a fiery brandy made from the same apples as the cider. It is used both as a digestif, and in the cooking of many regional dishes.

NORMANDIE

BONHOMME NORMAND
Duck with Cider and Cream

This recipe can also be used for pheasant or woodcock.

Metric/Imperial	American
1 × 1.75 kg/4 lb duck, trussed with thread or fine string	*1 × 4 lb duck, trussed with thread or fine string*
salt	*salt*
freshly ground black pepper	*freshly ground black pepper*
2 large rashers streaky bacon	*2 large slices fatty bacon*
100 g/4 oz butter	*½ cup butter*
750 g/1½ lb potatoes, peeled and quartered	*1½ lb potatoes, peeled and quartered*
2 tablespoons calvados, warmed	*2 tablespoons calvados, warmed*
200 ml/⅓ cup dry cider	*1 cup hard cider*
450 ml/¾ pint double cream	*2 cups heavy cream*

Sprinkle the inside of the duck lightly with salt and pepper. Put the bacon over the breast of the duck and tie in position with trussing thread or fine string.

Melt half the butter in a large flameproof roasting pan, add the duck and brown on all sides for about 10 minutes.

Cook, uncovered, in a preheated hot oven (220°C/425°F/Gas Mark 7) for 15 minutes. Lower the temperature to moderate (180°C/350°F/Gas Mark 4) and roast for a further 1 hour or until tender, basting occasionally.

Remove the duck from the pan and keep hot. Transfer the pan to the top of the stove, add the remaining butter and heat until melted. Add the potatoes and sauté for about 20 minutes until tender and golden, turning frequently.

CANARD À L'ORANGE

Duck with Orange

Metric/Imperial	American
75 g/3 oz butter	⅓ cup butter
1 × 2 kg/4 lb duck, trussed with thread or fine string	1 × 4 lb duck, trussed with thread or fine string
4 onions, peeled and sliced into thin rings	4 onions, peeled and sliced into thin rings
4 carrots, peeled and sliced into thin rings	4 carrots, peeled and sliced into thin rings
750 ml/1¼ pints dry white wine	3 cups dry white wine
1 bouquet garni★	1 bouquet garni★
salt	salt
freshly ground black pepper	freshly ground black pepper
2 oranges	2 oranges
1 teaspoon arrowroot	1 teaspoon arrowroot
juice of 2 oranges	juice of 2 oranges
1 teaspoon caster sugar	1 teaspoon sugar

Melt the butter in a large flameproof casserole, add the duck, onions and carrots and fry until the duck is golden brown on all sides, turning frequently.

Pour in the wine, bring to the boil and simmer for a few minutes until reduced slightly. Add the bouquet garni and salt and pepper to taste. Lower the heat, cover the casserole and simmer gently for 1½ hours or until the duck is tender, basting occasionally during cooking.

Meanwhile, finely pare the rind from the oranges, using a canelle knife or vegetable peeler to ensure none of the white pith is included. Cut the rind into fine strips, then plunge into a small pan of boiling water and blanch for 5 minutes. Drain, dry thoroughly on kitchen paper towels and set aside.

Cut the pared oranges into segments, removing the pith and skin which surrounds the segments. Set aside.

Remove the duck from the casserole and cut into serving pieces (wings, legs and thin slivers of breast meat). Place the duck on a plate, cover tightly, then stand the plate over a pan of hot water to keep the duck moist and hot.

Skim off excess fat from the cooking liquid, then strain. Pour 2 tablespoons of the liquid into a bowl, leave to cool, then mix to a paste with the arrowroot.

Pour the remaining cooking liquid into a heavy pan and reheat. Stir in the arrowroot paste, then simmer until the sauce thickens, stirring constantly. Remove from the heat, stir in the orange juice, sugar and blanched orange rind. Taste and adjust seasoning. Arrange the duck in the centre of a warmed serving platter and surround with the orange segments. Spoon the sauce over the duck and serve immediately.
SERVES 6

ABOVE: **Canard aux herbes; Canard à l'orange**
LEFT: **Bonhomme normand**

FAISANS EN BARBOUILLE

Pheasant Casserole with Mushrooms and Onions

Metric/Imperial
100 g/4 oz butter
4 carrots, peeled and thinly
   sliced
4 onions, peeled and thinly
   sliced
2 pheasants (about 2 kg/4 lb
   total weight), drawn and
   cut into 8 serving pieces
1 tablespoon plain flour
350 ml/12 fl oz good red
   wine
3 tablespoons brandy
7 tablespoons chicken stock
   (page 8)
salt
freshly ground black pepper
10 button mushrooms,
   thickly sliced

American
$\frac{1}{2}$ cup butter
4 carrots, peeled and thinly
   sliced
4 onions, peeled and thinly
   sliced
2 pheasants (about 4 lb total
   weight), drawn and cut
   into 8 serving pieces
1 tablespoon all-purpose
   flour
1$\frac{1}{2}$ cups good red wine
3 tablespoons brandy
7 tablespoons chicken stock
   (page 8)
salt
freshly ground black pepper
10 button mushrooms,
   thickly sliced

100 g/4 oz streaky bacon,
   rinds removed and cut
   into thin strips
10 small pickling onions,
   peeled

$\frac{1}{4}$ lb fatty bacon, sliced into
   thin strips
10 baby onions, peeled

Melt half the butter in a large flameproof casserole, add the carrots and onions and fry gently for a few minutes. Add the pieces of pheasant and fry until lightly coloured on all sides, then sprinkle in the flour and cook, stirring, until all the fat has been absorbed.

Pour in the wine, brandy, stock and a little salt and pepper to taste, then bring to the boil. Lower the heat, cover and simmer gently for 20 minutes.

Meanwhile, melt the remaining butter in a separate flameproof casserole. Add the mushrooms, bacon and onions and fry over brisk heat until lightly coloured. Remove the pheasant from its cooking liquid with a slotted spoon, then place in the casserole with the mushrooms, bacon and onions.

Strain the pheasant cooking liquid over the pheasant, stir well, then cover and simmer gently for a further 45 minutes or until the pheasants are tender. Taste and adjust the seasoning of the sauce. Serve immediately, straight from the casserole.
SERVES 8

LAPIN À L'AIL

Rabbit with Twenty Garlic Cloves

This recipe is a speciality of the Haut-Languedoc district, where it is also sometimes made with pork or tournedos steaks instead of the rabbit. If a whole rabbit is difficult to obtain, use fresh or frozen rabbit portions. For a milder garlic flavour, use only 12 garlic cloves.

Metric/Imperial
3 tablespoons oil
1 × 1.5 kg/3–$3\frac{1}{2}$ lb rabbit, trussed with thread or fine string, liver reserved
225 g/8 oz piece smoked bacon
20 garlic cloves
salt
freshly ground black pepper
150 ml/$\frac{1}{4}$ pint well-flavoured chicken stock (page 8)

American
3 tablespoons oil
1 × 3–$3\frac{1}{2}$ lb rabbit, trussed with thread or fine string, liver reserved
$\frac{1}{2}$ lb piece smoked bacon
20 garlic cloves
salt
freshly ground black pepper
$\frac{2}{3}$ cup well-flavored chicken stock (page 8)

Heat the oil in a large flameproof casserole, then put in the rabbit with the whole piece of bacon. Fry over brisk heat for about 10 minutes until lightly coloured on all sides.

Separate 10 garlic cloves, but do not peel them. Add them to the casserole, cover and cook over moderate heat for 10 minutes. Turn the rabbit over, sprinkle with salt and pepper to taste, then cover and cook for a further 10 minutes.

Peel the remaining garlic cloves and cut them in half lengthways. Remove the rabbit and bacon from the casserole, then add the halved garlic cloves and fry gently for a few minutes.

Return the rabbit and bacon to the casserole and cook over moderate heat for 10 minutes. Add the reserved rabbit liver and continue cooking for a further 10 to 20 minutes or until the rabbit is tender – the flesh should be white and fall away easily from the bones.

Remove the rabbit, bacon and liver. Cut the rabbit into serving pieces, the bacon and liver into thin strips. Keep hot.

Crush the garlic in the casserole with a wooden spoon, removing all the garlic skins which should come away easily. The garlic should be so soft that it mashes to a purée (paste). Stir the stock into this purée gradually, then simmer gently. Taste and adjust seasoning.

Place the rabbit in the centre of a warmed serving platter and surround with the strips of bacon and liver. Pour the sauce over the rabbit and serve immediately.
SERVES 4

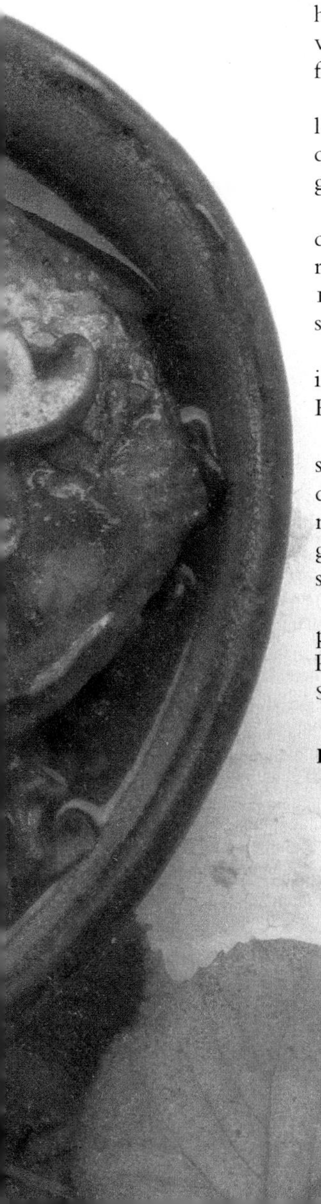

Faisans en barbouille

GIGUE DE CHEVREUIL

Pot-Roasted Venison

Metric/Imperial
1 × 1.5 kg/3–$3\frac{1}{2}$ lb leg of venison
5 tablespoons olive oil
leaves of 1 large rosemary sprig
6 shallots, peeled and sliced
2 carrots, peeled and sliced
2 onions, peeled and sliced
1 litre/$1\frac{3}{4}$ pints dry white wine
400 ml/14 fl oz red wine vinegar
*1 bouquet garni**
few juniper berries
salt
freshly ground black pepper
ground mixed spice
150 g/5 oz smoked fatty bacon, rind removed and cut into strips
100 g/4 oz butter
7 tablespoons hot water
40 g/$1\frac{1}{2}$ oz plain flour
2 teaspoons redcurrant jelly, to finish

American
1 × 3–$3\frac{1}{2}$ lb leg venison
5 tablespoons olive oil
leaves of 1 large rosemary sprig
6 scallions, peeled and sliced
2 carrots, peeled and sliced
2 onions, peeled and sliced
$4\frac{1}{4}$ cups dry white wine
$1\frac{3}{4}$ cups red wine vinegar
*1 bouquet garni**
few juniper berries
salt
freshly ground black pepper
ground allspice
ground cinnamon
5 oz smoked fatty bacon, cut into strips
$\frac{1}{2}$ cup butter
7 tablespoons hot water
$\frac{1}{3}$ cup all-purpose flour
2 teaspoons redcurrant jelly, to finish

Remove the outer membrane from the venison and any visible sinews and tendons. Rub the meat with 2 tablespoons oil, then roll it over the rosemary leaves so that they adhere to the meat.

Put half the shallots (scallions) in a large bowl with the carrots, onions, wine, half the wine vinegar, the remaining oil, the bouquet garni, juniper berries, and salt, pepper and spice(s) to taste.

Add the venison to this marinade, then leave in a cool place (not in the refrigerator) for 24 hours, turning the venison over from time to time.

The next day, remove the venison from the marinade and dry thoroughly on kitchen paper towels. Strain the marinade and reserve. Sew or lard the strips of fatty bacon into the venison.

Place the venison in a roasting pan and spread with two thirds of the butter. Roast in a preheated moderately hot oven (190°C/375°F/ Gas Mark 5) for $1\frac{1}{2}$ to $1\frac{3}{4}$ hours, basting the venison occasionally during cooking with the reserved marinade.

Halfway through the cooking time, sprinkle the meat with salt and pepper. Put the remaining shallots in a small heavy pan with the remaining wine vinegar. Boil rapidly until reduced by half, then add about 200 ml/$\frac{1}{3}$ pint/1 cup reserved marinade and the hot water. Stir well and simmer gently.

Meanwhile, melt the remaining butter in a separate pan, sprinkle in the flour and cook for 1 minute, stirring constantly. Stir in the shallot liquid gradually, stirring after each addition. Simmer until thick, then stir in the redcurrant jelly. Taste and adjust seasoning.

Transfer the venison to a warmed serving platter. Serve hot, with the sauce handed separately.
SERVES 6

MEATS

To understand meat cookery in France, it is almost essential to take a look in the window or chilling cabinet of a French butcher. To see the neatly trimmed steaks, escalopes and cutlets; the beautifully boned, rolled and larded joints, some with flavoursome stuffings; trays piled high with finely minced beef and veal; strings of white and black puddings, and bowls of creamy-white whipped lard.

Meat is expensive in France, but it is also of exceptionally high quality; thanks to the skill of the butcher, there is very little wastage. The French like to buy their meat ready-boned, trimmed and free from gristle and fat, and cut to the exact size for the dish that is to be cooked. These rules apply to both the prime and cheaper cuts of meat.

In France, braising, casseroling and stewing are popular cooking methods for the cheaper cuts. The meat is often marinated in wine or wine vinegar before cooking to help tenderize it; onions, garlic, herbs and seasonings are added for extra flavour. Before slow-cooking, the meat is usually fried quickly in hot fat or oil, to seal in the juices and give extra flavour to the finished dish. The choice of cooking vessel for casseroles and stews is also important. Cast iron and earthenware casserole dishes with tight-fitting lids are suitable, but a traditional French doufeu with an inverted lid is even better. Water is poured into the top of the lid to create steam so that the coarser, drier cuts of meat become moist during long, slow cooking in the oven.

Long, gentle cooking may be the preferred method for cooking cheaper cuts, but for roasting cuts the French prefer shorter cooking times. Often these times will seem incredibly short to those unused to French cooking – lamb in particular is always served pink. But taking into consideration that the meat is always of the highest quality, it is not surprising that the French prefer to appreciate its full flavour and succulence when underdone.

The French have their own very individual way of dividing a carcass and this sometimes makes it awkward or difficult to adapt French recipes. For this reason, the cuts of meat used in the recipes in this chapter have been adapted to the more usual cuts found in this country.

CAGHUSE
Pork with Onions

This simple dish is also called Kakusse in some regions of northern France. Although it is traditionally served cold, it is also excellent served hot.

Metric/Imperial	American
2 tablespoons saindoux★, pork dripping or butter	2 tablespoons saindoux★, pork drippings or butter
1.5 kg/3 lb leg of pork (fillet end)	3 lb leg of pork (fillet end)
6 medium onions, peeled and thickly sliced	6 medium onions, peeled and thickly sliced
salt	salt
freshly ground black pepper	freshly ground black pepper
2 tablespoons white wine vinegar	2 tablespoons white wine vinegar

Brush a baking dish or roasting pan with half the fat, then put in the pork. Sprinkle the onions around the pork, then sprinkle with salt and pepper to taste. Dot the pork and onions with the remaining fat.

Roast in a preheated moderate oven (160°C/325°F/ Gas Mark 3) for $2\frac{1}{4}$ to $2\frac{1}{2}$ hours or until the pork is tender, basting the pork with the cooking juices frequently during cooking.

Pour the wine vinegar into the onions and stir well to combine. Leave until cold before serving.
SERVES 4 TO 6

Porc au lait

RÔTI DE PORC AUX QUETSCHES

Roast Pork with Plums

Plums grow prolifically in Alsace–Lorraine, and the purple-skinned quetsch plums are the correct variety to use for this recipe. Golden mirabelle or any other variety of plum can be used instead of quetsch, but they may not need such a long cooking time. Braised cabbage is the traditional accompaniment.

Metric/Imperial	American
2 tablespoons saindoux★, pork dripping or butter	2 tablespoons saindoux★, pork drippings or butter
6 sage leaves, halved	6 sage leaves, halved
1.5 kg/3 lb boned and rolled loin or shoulder of pork	3 lb boned and rolled loin or shoulder of pork
salt	salt
freshly ground black pepper	freshly ground black pepper
2 tablespoons soft brown sugar	2 tablespoons soft brown sugar
7 tablespoons water	7 tablespoons water
1 kg/2 lb quetsch plums	2 lb quetsch plums

Brush a roasting pan with 1 tablespoon fat, then sprinkle with half the sage leaves. Put the pork in the pan, brush with the remaining fat, then sprinkle with salt and pepper and the remaining sage. Roast in a preheated moderately hot oven (190°C/375°F/Gas Mark 5) for 2 to 2¼ hours or until the pork is tender.

Fifteen minutes before the end of the cooking, put the sugar in a separate heavy pan with the water. Bring to the boil, add the plums and simmer gently for about 15 minutes, until tender but still whole.

Slice the pork neatly, then place in the centre of a warmed serving platter. Remove the plums from their cooking liquid with a slotted spoon and arrange around the edge of the platter. Drizzle a few spoons of the plum cooking liquid over the pork. Keep hot.

Boil the remaining plum cooking liquid for a few minutes, stirring constantly. Pour over the pork and plums or hand separately in a sauceboat. Serve immediately.

SERVES 4 TO 6

PORC AU LAIT

Pork Cooked in Milk

Metric/Imperial	American
1.5 kg/3 lb boned and rolled loin or shoulder of pork	3 lb boned and rolled loin or shoulder of pork
2 garlic cloves, peeled and cut into thin slivers	2 garlic cloves, peeled and cut into thin slivers
salt	salt
freshly ground black pepper	freshly ground black pepper
25 g/1 oz butter	2 tablespoons butter
1 thyme sprig	1 thyme sprig
1 bay leaf	1 bay leaf
1 litre/1¾ pints milk	4¼ cups milk

Make a few incisions in the pork with a sharp knife, then insert the slivers of garlic. Sprinkle with salt and pepper.

Melt the butter in a large flameproof casserole, add the pork and fry over moderate heat until browned on all sides. Add the thyme and bay leaf, then pour in the milk and bring slowly to the boil.

Cover and cook in a preheated moderate oven (160°C/325°F/Gas Mark 3) for 2¼ to 2½ hours or until the pork is tender, turning it over halfway during cooking.

Transfer the pork to a warmed serving dish. Discard the thyme and bay leaf and boil the milk rapidly for a few minutes to reduce slightly, then taste and adjust seasoning. Serve immediately, with the sauce handed separately in a sauceboat.

SERVES 4 TO 6

VARIATION: Add 150 ml/¼ pint/⅔ cup double (heavy) cream and 1 tablespoon prepared French mustard to the milk at the end of the cooking, then cook until reduced and thickened.

CAILLETTES
Pork and Spinach Patties

Caillettes are very similar to the better known crépinettes, often seen on French menus. Here they are served hot with a tomato sauce, but they are equally good served cold, in which case omit the tomato sauce and serve a tossed green salad instead.

Metric/Imperial	American
450 g/1 lb spinach, roughly chopped	1 lb spinach, roughly chopped
salt	salt
750 g/12 oz boned pork, minced	¾ lb boneless pork, ground
175 g/6 oz streaky bacon, rinds removed and minced	9 slices fatty bacon, ground
2 garlic cloves, peeled and crushed	2 garlic cloves, peeled and crushed
1 teaspoon dried thyme	1 teaspoon dried thyme
½ teaspoon dried marjoram	½ teaspoon dried marjoram
3 sage leaves, finely chopped	3 sage leaves, finely chopped
freshly ground black pepper	freshly ground black pepper
150 g/5 oz long-grain rice, boiled and drained	⅔ cup long-grain rice, boiled and drained
pig's caul casing★, soaked and drained	pig's caul casing★, soaked and drained
2 tablespoons olive oil	2 tablespoons olive oil
600 ml/1 pint tomato sauce (page 13), to serve	2½ cups tomato sauce (page 13), to serve

Put the spinach in a pan with just the water clinging to the leaves after washing, and a little salt. Cover and cook over brisk heat for 5 minutes until tender. Drain thoroughly and chop very finely.

Put the spinach in a bowl with the minced (ground) meat, bacon, garlic, herbs, and salt and pepper to taste. Mix well with the hands, then add the rice and mix until thoroughly combined.

Stretch out the pig's caul on a flat surface, then cut into six 15 cm/6 inch squares. Divide the meat and spinach mixture equally between the squares, placing it in the centre. Press the mixture flat and wrap the caul carefully around it.

Heat the oil in a frying pan (skillet). Place the *caillettes* in the pan and cook very gently for 1 hour, turning them over halfway during the cooking time. Serve hot, with the tomato sauce handed separately in a sauceboat.
SERVES 4 TO 6

PORC AUX POMMES
Pork with Apples

Metric/Imperial	American
1.5 kg/2 lb boned and rolled loin of pork	2 lb boned and rolled loin of pork
salt	salt
freshly ground black pepper	freshly ground black pepper
2 tablespoons water	2 tablespoons water
1 kg/2 lb cooking apples	2 lb tart apples
4 tablespoons dry cider	¼ cup hard cider
25 g/1 oz butter	2 tablespoons butter
2 tablespoons double cream	2 tablespoons heavy cream

Place the pork in a buttered roasting pan and sprinkle with salt and pepper. Add the water, then roast in a preheated moderately hot oven (190°C/375°F/Gas Mark 5) for 1¾ hours, basting frequently.

Peel and core the apples and slice into quarters. Remove the pork from the pan and drain off the cooking juices. Pour the cider into the pan, add the pork, then surround with the apples. Sprinkle with salt and pepper, then dot with the butter. Return to the moderately hot oven and roast for a further 20 minutes or until the pork is tender.

Transfer the pork to a warmed serving platter and surround with the apples. Stir the cream into the juices in the pan, then cook on top of the stove for 2 minutes, stirring constantly. Taste and adjust seasoning, then pour over the apples. Serve immediately.
SERVES 4 TO 6

Porc aux pommes; Côtes de porc aux lentilles

CÔTES DE PORC AUX LENTILLES

Pork Chops with Lentils

Metric/Imperial	American
450 g/1 lb green lentils	2 cups green lentils
1 bay leaf	1 bay leaf
2 onions, peeled	2 onions, peeled
1 whole clove	1 whole clove
salt	salt
freshly ground black pepper	freshly ground black pepper
6 pork chops, trimmed of fat	6 pork chops, trimmed of fat
4 sage leaves, chopped	4 sage leaves, chopped
50 g/2 oz saindoux★, pork dripping or butter	$\frac{1}{4}$ cup saindoux★, pork drippings or butter
6 small sausages★	6 small sausages★
2 carrots, peeled and diced	2 carrots, peeled and diced
about 600 ml/1 pint chicken stock (page 8)	about $2\frac{1}{2}$ cups chicken stock (page 8)

Rinse the lentils under cold running water and pick them over to remove any grit. Place in a large pan with the bay leaf and 1 onion stuck with the clove. Cover with water, bring to the boil and simmer for 1 hour. Add salt and pepper to taste halfway through the cooking time.

Meanwhile, sprinkle the chops with the sage and salt and pepper to taste. Melt the fat in a large flameproof casserole, add the chops and fry over brisk heat for 10 minutes until browned on all sides. Remove with a slotted spoon and set aside.

Prick the sausage skins with a fork. Chop the remaining onion. Add to the casserole with the carrots and fry over brisk heat for 10 minutes until lightly coloured, stirring constantly.

Drain the lentils, then add to the casserole with the chops. Cover with the stock and bring to the boil. Lower the heat, cover and cook gently for 1 hour or until the chops are tender.

Taste and adjust seasoning. Remove the chops and sausages from the casserole and arrange around the edge of a warmed serving platter. Pile the lentils in the centre. Serve immediately.

SERVES 6

ABOVE: **Echine de porc au raisin**
RIGHT: **Entrecôte Bercy**

CÔTES DE PORC VIGNERONNE

Pork Chops with Tomatoes and White Wine

The most suitable wine for this dish is Mâcon Blanc.

Metric/Imperial	American
6 pork chops, trimmed of fat	6 pork chops, trimmed of fat
salt	salt
freshly ground black pepper	freshly ground black pepper
2 tablespoons saindoux★, pork dripping or butter	2 tablespoons saindoux★, pork drippings or butter
4 ripe tomatoes, skinned and chopped	4 ripe tomatoes, skinned and chopped
200 ml/⅓ pint dry white wine	1 cup dry white wine
2 tablespoons Dijon-style mustard★	2 tablespoons Dijon-style mustard★
1 tablespoon snipped chives	1 tablespoon snipped chives
25 g/1 oz butter, softened	2 tablespoons butter

Sprinkle the chops with salt and pepper to taste. Melt the fat in a large frying pan (skillet), add the chops and fry over brisk heat until browned on all sides. Lower the heat, cover and cook gently for 45 minutes or until tender.

Meanwhile, purée the tomatoes in an electric blender or *mouli-legumes* (vegetable mill).

Transfer the chops to a warmed serving platter and keep hot. Pour the wine into the pan and stir to mix with the cooking juices and sediment. Add the puréed tomatoes, cook for 2 minutes, then remove from the heat and stir in the mustard and chives, and salt and pepper to taste. Whisk the butter into the sauce a little at a time, then pour over the chops. Serve immediately.
SERVES 6

ÉCHINE DE PORC AU RAISIN

Loin of Pork with Grapes

If you prefer a thick sauce to serve with the pork and grapes, mix 10 g/¼ oz/1½ teaspoons butter with 10 g/¼ oz/ 1 tablespoon plain (all-purpose) flour to make a beurre manie★. Whisk this into the sauce after adding the cream. Simmer until thick, whisking constantly.

Metric/Imperial	American
2 onions, peeled and sliced into rings	2 onions, peeled and sliced into rings
1 garlic clove, peeled and crushed	1 garlic clove, peeled and crushed
3 thyme sprigs	3 thyme sprigs
few rosemary leaves	few rosemary leaves
1 bay leaf	1 bay leaf
salt	salt
freshly ground black pepper	freshly ground black pepper
2 tablespoons oil	2 tablespoons oil
4 tablespoons marc or brandy	¼ cup marc or brandy
1.5 kg/3 lb boned and rolled loin of pork	3 lb boned and rolled loin of pork
25 g/1 oz butter	2 tablespoons butter
200 ml/⅓ pint dry white wine	1 cup dry white wine
1 kg/2 lb green grapes, peeled and seeded	2 lb green grapes, peeled and seeded
120 ml/4 fl oz double cream	½ cup heavy cream

Put the onions, garlic, thyme, rosemary and bay leaf in a large bowl with salt and pepper to taste. Stir in half the oil and the *marc* or brandy, then place the pork in the bowl. Turn the pork over several times in the marinade, then cover and leave to marinate for 2 to 3 hours.

Remove the pork from the marinade, drain and dry thoroughly on kitchen paper towels. Strain the marinade and reserve. Heat the remaining oil in a large flameproof casserole with the butter. Add the pork and fry over brisk heat until browned on all sides. Add the reserved marinade and the white wine and bring to the boil.

Lower the heat, cover and cook gently for 1½ to 2 hours or until the pork is tender. Add the grapes 5 minutes before the end of the cooking time.

Remove the pork from the casserole and slice neatly. Arrange on a warmed serving platter and keep hot. Stir the cream into the cooking liquid and simmer for 2 minutes, stirring constantly. Taste and adjust seasoning, then pour over the pork. Serve immediately.
SERVES 6

STEAK AUX OIGNONS

Rump Steak with Onions

If you like the flavour of fresh herbs with steak, they can be finely chopped and sprinkled over the dish just before serving. Parsley, chervil and tarragon go well with steak.

Metric/Imperial	American
25 g/1 oz butter	2 tablespoons butter
2 onions, peeled and thinly sliced	2 onions, peeled and thinly sliced
450 g/1 lb rump steak	1 lb top round steak
salt	salt
freshly ground black pepper	freshly ground black pepper
7 tablespoons dry white wine	7 tablespoons dry white wine
100 g/4 oz mushrooms, thinly sliced	1 cup thinly sliced mushrooms

Melt half the butter in a frying pan (skillet), add the onions and fry gently for 10 minutes.

Meanwhile, melt the remaining butter in a separate pan. Add the steak and cook over moderate heat for 3 to 6 minutes on each side, according to taste. Transfer to a warmed serving platter, sprinkle with salt and pepper and keep hot.

Stir the wine into the meat juices in the pan and scrape up any sediment. Add the mushrooms, increase the heat and cook rapidly until the liquid is glazed and reduced. Add salt and pepper to taste.

Sprinkle the steak with the onions, mushrooms and pan juices. Serve immediately.

SERVES 2 TO 3

ENTRECÔTE BERCY

Entrecôte (Sirloin) Steaks with Beurre Bercy

Metric/Imperial	American
BEURRE BERCY:	BEURRE BERCY:
1 beef marrow bone★ (about 175 g/6 oz in weight)	1 beef marrow bone★ (about 6 oz in weight)
salt	salt
120 ml/4 fl oz dry white wine	½ cup dry white wine
1 shallot, peeled and finely chopped	1 scallion, peeled and finely chopped
100 g/4 oz butter, softened	½ cup butter, softened
1 teaspoon lemon juice	1 teaspoon lemon juice
1 teaspoon chopped parsley	1 teaspoon chopped parsley
freshly ground black pepper	freshly ground black pepper
25 g/1 oz butter	2 tablespoons butter
1 tablespoon oil	1 tablespoon oil
4 entrecôte (sirloin) steaks, about 1 cm/½ inch thick	4 entrecôte (sirloin) steaks, about ½ inch thick

Make the *beurre Bercy* according to the method on page 50. Leave to cool.

Meanwhile, cook the steaks: Melt the butter in a heavy frying pan (skillet) with the oil. Add the steaks and fry for 3 to 5 minutes on each side, according to taste.

Sprinkle the steaks with salt and pepper, then transfer to a warmed serving platter. Top with the butter and serve immediately.

SERVES 4

In France, steaks are often cooked over a charcoal fire or barbecue, in which case they are brushed with 50 ml/2 fl oz/⅓ cup oil before cooking. They are usually served with *pommes frites* (French fries).

BOEUF BOURGUIGNON

Boeuf Bourguignon is excellent reheated, some say even better than when served the first time.

Metric/Imperial	American
1 large onion, peeled and thinly sliced	1 large onion, peeled and thinly sliced
1 parsley sprig	1 parsley sprig
1 thyme sprig, crumbled	1 thyme sprig, crumbled
1 bay leaf, crushed	1 bay leaf, crushed
1 kg/2 lb chuck steak or top rump, cut into large pieces	2 lb chuck steak or top round of beef, cut into large pieces
2 tablespoons marc or brandy	2 tablespoons marc or brandy
400 ml/14 fl oz red wine (preferably Bourgogne)	1¾ cups red wine (preferably Bourgogne)
2 tablespoons oil	2 tablespoons oil
50 g/2 oz butter	¼ cup butter
150 g/5 oz lean bacon, rind removed and cut into thin strips	⅔ cup lean bacon, cut into thin strips
24 small pickling onions, peeled	24 baby onions, peeled
450 g/1 lb button mushrooms, sliced	4 cups sliced button mushrooms
25 g/1 oz plain flour	¼ cup all-purpose flour
300 ml/½ pint beef stock (page 42)	1¼ cups beef stock (page 42)
1 garlic clove, peeled and crushed	1 garlic clove, peeled and crushed
1 bouquet garni★	1 bouquet garni★
salt	salt
freshly ground black pepper	freshly ground black pepper

Put a few onion slices in the bottom of a deep bowl with the parsley and a little of the thyme and bay leaf. Place a few pieces of beef on top. Continue with these layers until all the beef and herbs are used. Mix together the *marc* or brandy, wine and oil and pour over the beef. Cover and leave to marinate for at least 4 hours, stirring occasionally.

Melt the butter in a flameproof casserole, add the bacon and fry over moderate heat until golden brown. Remove with a slotted spoon and set aside. Add the small onions to the casserole and fry until lightly coloured on all sides, then remove with a slotted spoon and set aside. Add the mushrooms and fry, stirring, for 1 minute; drain.

Remove the pieces of beef from the marinade, then strain the marinade and set aside. Dry the beef thoroughly on kitchen paper towels, then add to the casserole and fry over brisk heat until browned on all sides. Sprinkle in the flour and cook, stirring, for 1 minute. Stir in the strained marinade gradually, then add the stock, garlic and bouquet garni. Add salt and pepper to taste, cover and simmer gently for 2 hours.

Skim off any fat on the surface of the cooking liquid. Add the bacon, onions and mushrooms, cover and simmer for 30 minutes or until the beef is tender.

Discard the bouquet garni, then taste and adjust seasoning. Transfer to a warmed serving dish and serve immediately.
SERVES 4 TO 6

CARBONNADES FLAMANDES

Flemish Carbonnade of Beef

Belgian beer is ideal for this recipe, but other beers may be used instead. Stout and dark beers are often used in carbonnades because they impart a rich flavour and dark colour. Half beer and half beef stock gives a lighter gravy.

Metric/Imperial	American
1 tablespoon saindoux★, dripping or butter	1 tablespoon saindoux★, drippings or butter
1 kg/2 lb chuck steak, cut into chunks	2 lb chuck steak, cut into chunks
450 g/1 lb onions, peeled and chopped	1 lb onions, peeled and chopped
1 tablespoon brown sugar	1 tablespoon brown sugar
2 tablespoons wine vinegar	2 tablespoons wine vinegar
salt	salt
freshly ground black pepper	freshly ground black pepper
1 bouquet garni★	1 bouquet garni★
1 large slice fresh bread, crust removed	1 large slice fresh bread, crust removed
2 tablespoons hot mustard★	2 tablespoons hot mustard★
about 600 ml/1 pint beer	about 2½ cups beer
2 tablespoons plain flour, for sealing	2 tablespoons all-purpose flour, for sealing
chopped parsley, to garnish	chopped parsley, for garnish

The secret of making a successful casserole lies in the choice of top quality ingredients. Prime beef suitable for long, slow cooking is obviously the essential ingredient, neither too fat and sinewy, nor too lean (chuck steak is the best cut to buy outside France). Use fresh vegetables and freshly picked herbs when available.

If stock is called for, use homemade stock. Stock cubes and boiling water will never impart the same richness of flavour. Good quality wine or beer should also be used.

ESTOUFFAT D'ARMAGNAC

Beef Casseroled in Wine with Armagnac

This dish is best made the day before required, so that the cooking liquid can become jellied and rich before reheating. No self-respecting French cook would make an estouffat without calf's (veal) foot★ and pork rinds★, since these are the ingredients that make the finished dish so rich in flavour. If you find they are difficult to obtain, omit them, but the end result will not be quite the same.

Metric/Imperial	American
1 calf's foot★, split	1 veal foot★, split
12 strips fresh pork rind★	12 strips fresh pork rind★
2 tablespoons saindoux★, dripping or butter	2 tablespoons saindoux★, drippings or butter
1 kg/2 lb stewing beef, cut into large pieces	2 lb stewing beef, cut into large pieces
225 g/8 oz shallots, peeled and chopped	2 cups chopped scallions
450 g/1 lb carrots, peeled and sliced into rings	1 lb carrots, peeled and sliced into rings
5 garlic cloves, peeled	5 garlic cloves, peeled
1 bouquet garni★	1 bouquet garni★
3 whole cloves	3 whole cloves
pinch of freshly grated nutmeg	pinch of freshly grated nutmeg
pinch of ground mixed spice	pinch of ground allspice
salt	pinch of ground cinnamon
freshly ground black pepper	salt
1 bottle red wine	freshly ground black pepper
50 ml/2 fl oz armagnac or brandy	1 bottle red wine
	$\frac{1}{3}$ cup armagnac or brandy

Melt the fat in a large flameproof casserole, add the beef and fry over brisk heat until browned on all sides. Remove with a slotted spoon and set aside.

Add the onions to the casserole and fry gently until soft and lightly coloured. Stir in the sugar and fry until the onions caramelize, then stir in the vinegar and scrape up all the sediment from the bottom of the casserole.

Return the beef to the casserole and mix with the onions. Add salt and pepper to taste, and the bouquet garni.

Spread one side of the bread with the mustard, then place on top of the beef and onions, mustard side down. Pour in enough beer to come just level with the bread.

Cover the casserole with a lid, then seal around the edge of the lid with a paste made from the flour and a few drops of water.

Cook in a preheated moderate oven (160°C/325°F/Gas Mark 3) for 2 hours. Break the paste seal, remove the lid, then discard the bread and bouquet garni. Taste and adjust seasoning, then transfer to a warmed deep serving dish and sprinkle with chopped parsley. Serve hot, with boiled potatoes and carrots or petits pois.
SERVES 4

Boeuf bourguignon; Carbonnades flamandes

Put the calf's (veal) foot in a pan, cover with water and bring to the boil. Boil for 15 minutes, then drain. Plunge the pork rinds into a pan of fresh boiling water to blanch them, then drain.

Melt the fat in a flameproof casserole. Add the beef, calf's foot, pork rinds, shallots (scallions), carrots, garlic and bouquet garni. Add the cloves, nutmeg, spice(s), and salt and pepper to taste. Pour in the wine and bring to the boil.

Cover with a tight-fitting lid, transfer to a preheated cool oven (140°C/275°F/Gas Mark 1) and cook for about 3 hours. Transfer the casserole to the top of the stove and stir in the *armagnac* or brandy. Simmer gently for 30 minutes.

To serve, place the beef in a warmed deep serving dish, taking great care to keep the pieces whole as they will be very tender. Keep hot.

Remove the bones from the calf's foot and dice the meat. Cut the pork rinds into very thin strips. Surround the beef with the calf's foot and pork rinds. Discard the garlic and bouquet garni from the cooking liquor, then taste and adjust seasoning. Pour over the beef.
SERVES 4 TO 6

VARIATION: In the Béarn region, *estouffat* is made with diced raw ham★ as well as beef, and slices of streaky (fatty) bacon are placed on top of the casserole before placing it in the oven.

POT-AU-FEU

This famous dish is cooked throughout France, and each region has its own variation. It is really two dishes in one, because the cooking liquid or broth is served as a soup, then the meats and vegetables follow as the main course. The marrow from the beef bones is usually poured over baked bread which is served with the broth, although in this particular recipe the marrow bones are served along with the meats and vegetables. Accompaniments to the beef include mustard, horseradish, capers and gherkins (sweet dill pickles). A vinaigrette dressing (page 13) is sometimes poured over the vegetables just before serving.

A good pot-au-feu depends on very slow, even cooking. The cooking liquid should barely simmer.

Metric/Imperial	American
750 g/1½–1¾ lb flank of beef, in one piece	1½–1¾ lb flank of beef, in one piece
750 g/1½–1¾ lb silverside, in one piece	1½–1¾ lb silverside, in one piece
750 g/1½–1¾ lb shin of beef, in one piece	1½–1¾ lb shin of beef, in one piece
3 litres/5½ pints water	6½ pints water
2 onions, peeled and stuck with 4 whole cloves	2 onions, peeled and stuck with 4 cloves
1 bouquet garni★	1 bouquet garni★
4 garlic cloves	4 garlic cloves
1 tablespoon coarse sea salt	1 tablespoon coarse sea salt
12 black peppercorns	12 black peppercorns
1 bunch celery, trimmed, separated into sticks, then tied in a bundle	1 bunch celery, trimmed, separated into stalks, then tied in a bundle
4 leeks (white part only), tied in a bundle	4 leeks (white part only), tied in a bundle
12 young carrots, peeled	12 young carrots, peeled
8 small turnips, peeled	8 small turnips, peeled
8 potatoes, scrubbed	8 potatoes, scrubbed
4 pieces beef marrow bone★ (about 7.5 cm/3 inches long)	4 pieces beef marrow bone★ (about 3 inches long)
salt	salt

Tie the pieces of meat securely with string. Put the beef flank in a very large flameproof *pot-au-feu, marmite* or casserole. Pour in the water, then bring slowly to the boil. Skim off the scum, then lower the heat and simmer very gently for 1 hour, skimming occasionally.

Add the silverside, shin, onions, bouquet garni, unpeeled garlic cloves, sea salt and peppercorns. Bring to the boil and skim the surface again, then lower the heat and simmer gently, uncovered, for a further 1 hour.

Add the celery, leeks, carrots and turnips at 10 minute intervals, do not add them all at the same time as this will lower the temperature of the *pot-au-feu*. Continue simmering until the total cooking time is 4 hours, then remove from the heat and leave to stand for 15 minutes.

Meanwhile, cook the unpeeled potatoes in a separate pan of boiling water for 20 minutes until tender. Put the beef marrow bones in another pan, cover with cold salted water and bring to the boil. Simmer for 15 minutes.

Remove the meats and vegetables from the stock and discard all bones and string. Place the meats and vegetables in a warmed serving dish. Peel the potatoes while still warm, then add to the dish with the drained marrow bones. Sprinkle a little of the hot stock over the meats and vegetables; keep hot.

Degrease★ the stock, then pass through a sieve (strainer) lined with damp muslin (cheesecloth). Reheat the stock if necessary, then taste and adjust seasoning. Serve the stock hot as a soup, followed by the hot meat and vegetables for the main course.
SERVES 8

Pot-au-feu

FRAGINAT DE BOEUF À LA CATALANE

Beef Casserole with Aïoli

The usual accompaniment to this dish is boiled rice. Make the tomato purée by puréeing skinned and seeded tomatoes in a mouli-légumes (vegetable mill) or an electric blender.

Metric/Imperial
2 tablespoons saindoux★, dripping or butter
1 kg/2 lb chuck steak, cut into chunks
6 garlic cloves, peeled and crushed
1–2 tablespoons chopped parsley
1 tablespoon plain flour
250 ml/8 fl oz fresh tomato purée
freshly grated nutmeg
salt
freshly ground black pepper
450 g/1 lb small pickling onions, peeled
250 ml/8 fl oz aïoli (page 14)
3–4 tablespoons lukewarm water

American
2 tablespoons saindoux★, drippings or butter
2 lb chuck steak, cut into chunks
6 garlic cloves, peeled and crushed
1–2 tablespoons chopped parsley
1 tablespoon all-purpose flour
1 cup fresh tomato purée
freshly grated nutmeg
salt
freshly ground black pepper
1 lb baby onions, peeled
1 cup aïoli (page 14)
3–4 tablespoons lukewarm water

Melt half the fat in a flameproof casserole. Add the beef and fry over moderate heat until the juices run. Pour off the pan juices into a bowl and reserve.

Melt the remaining fat in the casserole. Mix the garlic and parsley together to make an *hachis*. Add to the casserole and fry over brisk heat for about 5 minutes, stirring constantly.

Sprinkle in the flour, cook for 1 minute, stirring constantly, then stir in the tomato purée and bring to the boil. Add nutmeg, salt and pepper to taste, lower the heat, cover and simmer gently for 1½ hours.

Stir in the whole onions and simmer for a further 40 minutes or until the beef is tender. Meanwhile, mix the *aïoli* and warm water together and stir in the reserved pan juices from the beef.

Remove the beef from the cooking liquid with a slotted spoon and place in a warmed serving dish. Keep hot. Remove the casserole from the heat and stir the *aïoli* gradually into the cooking liquid. Taste and adjust seasoning. Serve the beef immediately, with the sauce handed separately.
SERVES 4 TO 6

AGNEAU RÔTI DE PAUILLAC

Roast Leg of Lamb with Potatoes

Metric/Imperial	American
1 × 2 kg/4 lb leg of lamb	1 × 4 lb leg of lamb
8 garlic cloves, peeled	8 garlic cloves, peeled
50 g/2 oz butter, softened	$\frac{1}{4}$ cup softened butter
2 handfuls dried breadcrumbs	2 handfuls dried bread crumbs
4 tablespoons finely chopped parsley	$\frac{1}{4}$ cup finely chopped parsley
salt	salt
freshly ground black pepper	freshly ground black pepper
4 tablespoons oil	$\frac{1}{4}$ cup oil
1.5 kg/3–3$\frac{1}{2}$ lb new potatoes, peeled and sliced into thin rounds	3–3$\frac{1}{2}$ lb new potatoes, peeled and sliced into thin rounds
TO DEGLAZE:	TO DEGLAZE:
7 tablespoons wine vinegar	7 tablespoons wine vinegar
3 garlic cloves, peeled and crushed	3 garlic cloves, peeled and crushed
5 tablespoons boiling water	5 tablespoons boiling water

Place the lamb in a roasting pan. Cut two garlic cloves into quarters. Make 2 slits in the lamb alongside the bone with a sharp knife and insert a quarter of a garlic clove into each slit. Push the remaining quarters into the skin of the lamb. Spread the butter all over the lamb.

Crush the remaining 6 garlic cloves, then make a *hachis* by mixing them with the breadcrumbs, parsley, and salt and pepper to taste. Spread this *hachis* evenly over the lamb, then roast in a preheated moderately hot oven (200°C/400°F/Gas Mark 6) for 1$\frac{3}{4}$ to 2 hours, or according to your liking.

Meanwhile, heat the oil in a large frying pan (skillet). Add the potatoes and fry over brisk heat for a few minutes. Lower the heat, cover the pan and cook gently for 10 minutes or until the potatoes are golden brown on the underside. Turn the potatoes over with a spatula and cook the other side until tender.

Remove the lamb from the oven and carve into neat slices. Arrange the slices in a circle on a warmed serving platter. Remove the potatoes from the heat, sprinkle with salt and pepper, then pile onto the serving platter. Keep hot.

To deglaze★: boil the wine vinegar with the crushed garlic until reduced to one quarter of its original volume. Strain, add the boiling water and stir into the juices in the roasting pan, scraping up all the sediment and juices from the bottom. Pour into a sauceboat and serve hot, with the lamb.
SERVES 6

VARIATION: The potatoes can be sprinkled with the same *hachis* as the lamb, to give them extra flavour.

MOUTON GARDIANNE

Lamb Chops with Potatoes and Garlic

Metric/Imperial	American
2 tablespoons olive oil	2 tablespoons olive oil
4 large lamb chops, trimmed of fat	4 large lamb chops, trimmed of fat
4 potatoes, peeled and sliced into thick rounds	4 potatoes, peeled and sliced into thick rounds
3 garlic cloves, peeled and crushed	3 garlic cloves, peeled and crushed
2 thyme sprigs	2 thyme sprigs
1 bay leaf	1 bay leaf
1 rosemary sprig	1 rosemary sprig
salt	salt
freshly ground black pepper	freshly ground black pepper
about 300 ml/$\frac{1}{2}$ pint boiling hot beef stock (page 8)	about 1$\frac{1}{4}$ cups boiling hot beef stock (page 8)
1 tablespoon chopped parsley	1 tablespoon chopped parsley

Heat the oil in a large frying pan (skillet), add the chops and fry over brisk heat until browned on both sides. Remove from the pan and set aside.

Lower the heat and add the potatoes to the pan. Sprinkle with the garlic, then add the thyme, bay leaf and rosemary, and salt and pepper to taste. Place the chops on top and pour in enough stock to just cover.

Cook over brisk heat for about 40 minutes or until the lamb is tender. Press the chops into the potatoes occasionally to crush them to a purée.

Serve hot straight from the pan, sprinkled with the parsley.
SERVES 4

Gigot à la bretonne;
Agneau rôti de pauillac

GIGOT À LA BRETONNE

Leg of Lamb with White Haricot (Navy) Beans

Metric/Imperial	American
1 × 2 kg/4 lb leg of lamb	1 × 4 lb leg of lamb
4 tablespoons olive oil	¼ cup olive oil
salt	salt
freshly ground black pepper	freshly ground black pepper
450 g/1 lb dried white haricot beans, soaked overnight in cold water	2¼ cups dried navy beans, soaked overnight in cold water
3 onions, peeled	3 onions, peeled
1 whole clove	1 whole clove
1 bouquet garni★	1 bouquet garni★
1 garlic clove, peeled and chopped	1 garlic clove, peeled and chopped
3 tomatoes, skinned and roughly chopped	3 tomatoes, skinned and roughly chopped
25 g/1 oz butter, softened	2 tablespoons softened butter

Place the lamb in a roasting pan, then sprinkle with half the oil and salt and pepper to taste. Roast in a preheated moderately hot oven (200°C/400°F/Gas Mark 6) for 1¾ to 2 hours, or according to your liking.

Meanwhile, drain the haricots, rinse under cold running water, then place in a large pan and cover with fresh water. Add 1 onion stuck with the clove and the bouquet garni. Bring to the boil, then lower the heat, cover and simmer for 45 minutes to 1 hour until tender. Add salt to taste halfway through the cooking time.

Chop the remaining onions. Heat the remaining oil in a heavy pan, add the chopped onions and fry gently for 10 minutes. Add the garlic and tomatoes, and salt and pepper to taste, then cook gently until thick.

When the beans are tender, drain and discard the onion, clove and bouquet garni. Add the beans to the tomato mixture with the butter and stir well to mix. Heat through gently, then taste and adjust seasoning.

Place the lamb on a warmed serving platter and surround with the beans and tomatoes. Deglaze★ the juices in the roasting pan with a little boiling water, then pour into a sauceboat. Serve hot.
SERVES 6

FOIE DE VEAU À LA LYONNAISE

Calf's (Veal) Liver with Onions

Metric/Imperial	American
450 g/1 lb calf's liver, sliced	1 lb veal liver, sliced
salt	salt
freshly ground black pepper	freshly ground black pepper
2 tablespoons plain flour	2 tablespoons all-purpose flour
50 g/2 oz butter	$\frac{1}{4}$ cup butter
4 onions, peeled and thinly sliced	4 onions, peeled and thinly sliced
2 tablespoons wine vinegar	2 tablespoons wine vinegar
chopped parsley, to garnish (optional)	chopped parsley, for garnish (optional)

Sprinkle the liver with salt and pepper to taste, then coat in the flour, shaking off the excess.

Melt half the butter in a frying pan (skillet), add the liver and fry over brisk heat for 2 minutes on each side. Transfer to a warmed serving platter and keep hot.

Melt the remaining butter in the pan. Add the onions and fry over very gentle heat until soft and lightly coloured, stirring frequently. Stir in the vinegar, and salt and pepper to taste.

Sprinkle the onions over the liver, then garnish with parsley, if liked. Serve immediately.
SERVES 4

LANGUE DE BOEUF SAUCE PIQUANTE

Calf's (Veal) Tongue with Piquant Sauce

Metric/Imperial	American
1 calf's tongue, dressed	1 veal tongue, dressed
2 carrots, peeled and sliced into rings	2 carrots, peeled and sliced into rings
2 leeks (white part only), sliced	2 leeks (white part only), sliced
2 onions, peeled and sliced into rings	2 onions, peeled and sliced into rings
2.5 litres/4½ pints water	5½ pints (11 cups) water
salt	salt
few black peppercorns	few black peppercorns
1 bouquet garni★	1 bouquet garni★
2 shallots, peeled and chopped	2 scallions, peeled and chopped
4 tablespoons wine vinegar	$\frac{1}{4}$ cup wine vinegar
1 tablespoon butter	1 tablespoon butter
1 tablespoon plain flour	1 tablespoon all-purpose flour
4 gherkins, diced	4 small dill pickles, diced
freshly ground black pepper	freshly ground black pepper

Put the tongue in a large pan, cover with cold water and bring to the boil. Boil for 20 minutes, skimming occasionally with a slotted spoon, then drain and rinse under cold running water.

Put the vegetables in a pan with the measured water, salt, peppercorns and bouquet garni. Bring to the boil, add the tongue and simmer for 3 hours or until tender.

Put the shallots (scallions) and wine vinegar in a separate small pan and boil rapidly until all the vinegar has evaporated.

Meanwhile, melt the butter in another pan. Sprinkle in the flour and cook, stirring, for 1 minute to obtain a smooth *roux* (paste). Gradually stir in about 300 ml/ $\frac{1}{2}$ pint/1$\frac{1}{4}$ cups of the boiling stock from the tongue. Bring slowly to the boil, stirring constantly, then add the shallots and gherkins (dill pickles), and salt and pepper to taste. Lower the heat and simmer for 5 to 6 minutes until thick, stirring frequently.

Drain the tongue and remove the outer skin. Slice the meat neatly, then place on a warmed serving platter. Pour over the sauce and serve immediately.
SERVES 8

RIS DE VEAU À LA NORMANDE

Calf's (Veal) Sweetbreads with Mushrooms and Cream

Metric/Imperial	American
4 calf's sweetbreads	4 veal sweetbreads, trimmed and sliced
150 g/5 oz butter	$\frac{2}{3}$ cup butter
225 g/8 oz mushrooms, trimmed and sliced	2 cups trimmed and sliced mushrooms
2 tablespoons plain flour	2 tablespoons all-purpose flour
salt	salt
freshly ground black pepper	freshly ground black pepper
7 tablespoons calvados or brandy	7 tablespoons calvados or brandy
200 ml/$\frac{1}{3}$ pint double cream	1 cup heavy cream

Soak the sweetbreads in cold water for 3 hours, changing the water 2 or 3 times. Drain the sweetbreads and rinse thoroughly under cold running water. Place them in a pan, cover with fresh water, then bring slowly to the boil. Simmer for 5 minutes, then drain and rinse again under cold running water. Remove any fatty parts, then place the sweetbreads between 2 plates and weight them down. Leave for 1 hour.

Melt half the butter in a frying pan (skillet). Slice the sweetbreads and add to the pan. Fry over gentle heat until lightly coloured on both sides.

Coat the mushrooms in the flour, shaking off the excess. Add the mushrooms to the pan, sprinkle with salt and pepper to taste, then cover and simmer very gently for 15 minutes. Remove the sweetbreads and mushrooms from the pan with a slotted spoon and place on a warmed serving platter. Keep hot.

Stir the *calvados* or brandy into the pan and scrape up the sediment from the bottom. Stir in the cream and simmer until reduced by half. Remove from the heat, then add the remaining butter a little at a time, whisking vigorously. Taste and adjust seasoning, then pour over the sweetbreads. Serve immediately.

SERVES 4

Foie de veau à la lyonnaise; Andouillettes au Vouvray

ANDOUILLETTES AU VOUVRAY

Sausages and Mushrooms with White Wine

Andouillettes are spicy sausages made from tripe or chitterlings. They are very popular in France, and can be found in almost every charcuterie there. Outside France they may occasionally be found in good French delicatessens or speciality shops, but if they are difficult to obtain, this dish can equally well be made with any other French sausage.
Only use the still Vouvray wine in cooking, not the sparkling variety. The usual accompaniment to a dish of andouillettes is creamed sorrel or spinach.

Metric/Imperial	American
2 tablespoons saindoux★, dripping or butter	2 tablespoons saindoux★, drippings or butter
6 andouillettes★, sliced	6 andouillettes★, sliced
3 shallots, peeled and chopped	3 scallions, peeled and chopped
225 g/8 oz mushrooms, sliced	2–2¼ cups sliced mushrooms
300 ml/½ pint Vouvray (dry white) wine	1¼ cups Vouvray (dry white) wine
salt	salt
freshly ground black pepper	freshly ground black pepper
2 tablespoons dried breadcrumbs	2 tablespoons dried bread crumbs

Melt half the fat in a frying pan (skillet), add the sausage and fry over moderate heat until golden brown and crisp. Pour a little of the cooking fat onto a heatproof serving platter, then arrange the sausage on the platter. Keep hot.

Add the shallots (scallions) to the pan and fry until lightly coloured. Add the mushrooms and fry until their juices run. Pour in the wine and add salt and pepper to taste. Cover and cook gently for 15 minutes.

Pour the mushroom mixture over the sausages, then sprinkle with the breadcrumbs and dot with the remaining fat. Put under a preheated hot grill (broiler) until the topping is golden brown. Serve immediately.

SERVES 6

VEGETABLES

To the French, vegetables are as important a part of the meal as the meat, fish, eggs or cheese, for rarely are they served simply as an accompaniment to a main course. Vegetables are a dish in their own right, and as much attention goes into their preparation and cooking as it does into any other part of the meal. Apart from their use in hors d'oeuvre dishes, the usual custom is to serve vegetables after the main dish of meat or fish, etc., so they can be appreciated on their own rather than being mixed with – and spoilt by – the sauces and gravies from other dishes.

French cooking methods for vegetables are different, but perhaps the main difference lies in the freshness and quality of the vegetables themselves. In France, vegetables are picked young and small. Courgettes (zucchini), for example, are never allowed to grow to the size of marrows (squash) in the way they are in other countries. They are picked while still tiny, sweet and full of flavour; the same rule applies to all the different types of beans and root vegetables – such as carrots, turnips and parsnips. But perhaps most important of all, they are eaten while still fresh, as soon as possible after picking, for the French housewife invariably buys her vegetables daily from the local vegetable market. Not for her the frozen vegetables available all year round, she prefers to use only fresh vegetables in season.

In order to make full use of each vegetable in season, the French have invented numerous ways of preparing and cooking each one, so that it is impossible to tire of them. Potato dishes are a fine example of French ingenuity, for there are literally hundreds of different ways to cook and serve them, each one deliciously different from the other.

Contrary to what you might expect, simplicity is always the keynote when cooking vegetables. First and foremost, it is essential to banish all thought of boiling vegetables in copious amounts of water. In France, if vegetables are to be boiled at all, they are simply thrown into a pan containing the minimum amount of boiling water, brought quickly back to the boil, then boiled briskly; the cooking time should be just sufficient to take away rawness, yet at the same time retain crispness. After draining, they are refreshed in a strainer held under cold running water, then left until the moment of serving when they can be quickly tossed in melted butter over moderate heat until heated through.

An equally popular method for cooking vegetables à la française is to braise or sweat them in a small amount of stock. This can be done on top of the stove or in the oven; the secret is to have a heavy-based pan (cast iron is best) with a tight-fitting lid so that the moisture from the vegetables is retained in the pan, then served with them. Glazing takes this method one step further, by adding sugar and sometimes butter to the stock. During cooking, the vegetable becomes coated in a sweet, shiny glaze – this is a favourite method for root vegetables, particularly carrots.

ARTICHAUTS À LA BARIGOULE
Artichokes Cooked in Wine with Garlic

In Provence, the small violet-coloured artichokes are always used for this dish, but any very young and tender artichokes will be suitable. The original recipe for artichauts à la barigoule is believed to be one of the oldest of Provençal dishes; in it the artichokes were cut in half lengthways, then brushed with oil and grilled (broiled). This is a more modern version.

Metric/Imperial	American
6 small globe artichokes	6 small globe artichokes
7 tablespoons oil	7 tablespoons oil
2 onions, peeled and chopped	2 onions, peeled and chopped
2 carrots, peeled and diced	2 carrots, peeled and diced
salt	salt
freshly ground black pepper	freshly ground black pepper
200 ml/$\frac{1}{3}$ pint dry white wine	1 cup dry white wine
2 garlic cloves, peeled and crushed	2 garlic cloves, peeled and crushed
7 tablespoons water	7 tablespoons water

ARTICHAUTS À LA LANGUEDOCIENNE
Artichokes with Pork, Ham and Wine

The perfect artichokes for this recipe are the very small violet-coloured variety which are most often sold in bunches. If only larger ones are obtainable, blanch them for a few minutes in boiling water to which a few drops of lemon juice have been added, then follow the recipe as for the small ones. In the Languedoc region, these artichokes are the traditional accompaniment to grilled (broiled) lamb cutlets.

Metric/Imperial	American
12 small globe artichokes	*12 small globe artichokes*
2 lemons	*2 lemons*
3 tablespoons olive oil	*3 tablespoons olive oil*
1 onion, peeled and chopped	*1 onion, peeled and chopped*
1 shallot, peeled and chopped	*1 scallion, peeled and chopped*
75 g/3 oz belly pork, diced	*$\frac{1}{3}$ cup diced pork sides*
100 g/4 oz raw ham★, diced	*$\frac{1}{2}$ cup diced raw ham★*
1 tablespoon plain flour	*1 tablespoon all-purpose flour*
750 ml/1$\frac{1}{4}$ pints dry white wine	*3 cups dry white wine*
little light stock or water, if necessary	*little light stock or water, if necessary*
freshly ground black pepper	*freshly ground black pepper*

Remove the hard outer leaves from the artichokes. Trim all the stalks to the same short length. Cut the tips off the remaining leaves with scissors. Cut the artichokes in quarters lengthways and scoop out the chokes with a sharp teaspoon.

Rub the cut surfaces of the artichokes with one of the lemons cut in half, then place in a bowl of cold water with the juice of the remaining lemon.

Heat the oil in a large heavy pan, add the onion and shallot (scallion) and fry gently until soft but not coloured. Add the pork and ham and fry for a further 5 minutes, stirring frequently.

Add the artichokes and fry gently for 10 minutes, stirring occasionally. Sprinkle in the flour and cook for 1 minute, stirring well to absorb all the fat in the pan.

Pour in the wine to just cover the artichokes, adding a little stock or water if there is not enough wine. Add pepper to taste, then cover and simmer for 30 minutes or until the artichokes are very tender. Transfer to a warmed serving dish. Serve hot.
SERVES 6

VARIATION: In Catalonia the artichokes are sprinkled with a *hachis* of breadcrumbs, garlic, parsley and belly pork, before cooking without liquid.

Remove the hard outer leaves from the artichokes. Trim all the stalks to the same short length. Cut the tips off the remaining leaves with scissors and scoop out the chokes with a sharp teaspoon. Plunge the artichokes into a bowl of cold water and wash them thoroughly, prising the leaves apart so that the water penetrates deep into the base of the leaves. Drain the artichokes thoroughly by standing them upside down in a colander.

Pour half the oil into a deep flameproof casserole, then make a layer of the onions and carrots in the bottom. Place the artichokes on top, leaves uppermost, then sprinkle with salt and pepper to taste and the remaining oil.

Cover the casserole and cook over moderate heat for 15 minutes, shaking the pan occasionally and making sure that the onions and carrots do not burn.

Pour in the wine, increase the heat and boil uncovered until the liquid has reduced by one third. Add the garlic and water, cover the casserole again, then cook over moderate heat for 40 minutes or until the artichokes are very tender and the liquid is almost completely absorbed. Transfer to a warmed serving dish. Serve hot.
SERVES 3

Artichauts à la languedocienne

Farcun rouergat; Petits
pois à la vendéene

PÉRIGORD

FARCUN ROUERGAT

Spinach and Ham in Béchamel Sauce

*In the original recipe, the mixture is covered during baking,
with a piece of pig's caul to add flavour. It is not essential,
but if you use one, soak it in lukewarm water before use.*

Metric/Imperial	American
1 kg/2 lb spinach, thinly sliced	*2 lb spinach, thinly sliced*
2 celery sticks, thinly sliced	*2 celery stalks, thinly sliced*
4 garlic cloves, peeled and finely chopped	*4 garlic cloves, peeled and finely chopped*
225 g/8 oz ham★, finely chopped	*1 cup finely chopped ham★*
2 parsley sprigs, finely chopped	*2 parsley sprigs, finely chopped*
2 thyme sprigs	*2 thyme sprigs*
freshly ground black pepper	*freshly ground black pepper*
25 g/1 oz butter	*2 tablespoons butter*
25 g/1 oz plain flour	*¼ cup all-purpose flour*
600 ml/1 pint milk	*2½ cups milk*
freshly grated nutmeg	*freshly grated nutmeg*
salt	*salt*
1 egg	*1 egg*
100 ml/4 fl oz double cream	*½ cup heavy cream*

Put the spinach in a bowl with the celery, garlic, ham
and parsley. Rub the leaves from the thyme between
your fingers over the bowl, add pepper to taste, then
mix the ingredients well together.

Melt the butter in a heavy pan, sprinkle in the flour
and cook, stirring constantly, for 1 minute to obtain a
smooth *roux* (paste). Remove from the heat and add
the milk gradually, stirring vigorously after each
addition. Bring slowly to the boil, stirring constantly,
then lower the heat and simmer, stirring, for 3 to 4
minutes. Add nutmeg, salt and pepper to taste, then
remove from the heat.

Whisk the egg and cream together, then slowly stir
into the sauce. Fold the vegetable mixture into the
sauce until thoroughly incorporated.

Pour the mixture into a buttered gratin dish and
level the surface. Cover with a lid and bake in a
preheated moderate oven (160°C/325°F/Gas Mark 3)
for 20 to 25 minutes. Serve hot, straight from the
dish.

SERVES 4 TO 6

CHOU AU LARD

White Cabbage with Bacon

Metric/Imperial	American
150 g/5 oz streaky bacon, rind removed and chopped	⅔ cup finely chopped fatty bacon
2 tablespoons red wine vinegar	2 tablespoons red wine vinegar
1 white cabbage, cored and shredded	1 white cabbage, cored and shredded
salt	salt
freshly ground black pepper	freshly ground black pepper

Put the bacon in a heavy pan and cook over moderate heat until the fat runs. Remove from the heat and add the wine vinegar.

Add the cabbage to the pan with salt and pepper to taste. Fry over high heat for 3 to 4 minutes, shaking the pan vigorously to mix the ingredients together. Serve immediately.

SERVES 4

PAPETON D'AUBERGINES

Aubergines (Eggplant) Baked with Parmesan and Eggs

This dish is usually served hot with a homemade tomato sauce (page 13), but it is equally good served cold, in which case it should be left to cool in the baking dish, then unmoulded before serving.

Metric/Imperial	American
7 tablespoons olive oil	7 tablespoons olive oil
1.5 kg/3–3½ lb aubergines, diced	3–3½ lb eggplant, diced
2 thyme sprigs	2 thyme sprigs
salt	salt
freshly ground black pepper	freshly ground black pepper
1 garlic clove, peeled and crushed	1 garlic clove, peeled and crushed
75 g/3 oz Parmesan cheese, grated	¾ cup grated Parmesan cheese
4 eggs, beaten	4 eggs, beaten

Heat the oil in a heavy pan, add the aubergines (eggplant) and fry over moderate heat for 20 minutes.

Work the aubergines and thyme leaves through the medium blade of a *mouli-légumes* (vegetable mill) or purée in an electric blender. Season with salt and pepper to taste. Add the garlic, Parmesan and eggs and beat well to mix.

Pour the mixture into an oiled baking dish, then bake in a preheated moderately hot oven (200°C/400°F/Gas Mark 6) for 20 to 30 minutes. The top of the *papeton* should be golden brown. Serve hot, straight from the baking dish.

SERVES 6

Sprigs of fresh thyme are used frequently in French recipes, not only as part of the traditional bouquet garni, but also as a flavouring in their own right. Thyme is an essential herb in the Provençal mixture of dried herbs known as *herbes du midi* or *herbès du Provence*. It is a selection of Mediterranean herbs, impossible to imitate elsewhere, but sachets and pots are available at specialist shops. The flavour of thyme goes well with most green vegetable dishes, and with carrots. A sprig kept in a bottle of wine vinegar gives the vinegar a subtle flavour of thyme, perfect for vinaigrette.

PETITS POIS À LA VENDÉENNE

Petits Pois with Onions, Herbs and Lettuce

Metric/Imperial	American
50 g/2 oz butter	¼ cup butter
1 kg/2 lb petits pois, shelled	2 lb petits pois, shelled
12 small pickling onions, peeled	12 baby onions, peeled
finely chopped parsley, savory and thyme, to taste	finely chopped parsley, savory and thyme to taste
1 lettuce heart	1 lettuce heart
2 pinches of sugar	2 pinches of sugar
salt	salt
freshly ground black pepper	freshly ground black pepper

Melt the butter in a pan and add the peas, onions and herbs. Cook gently for 10 minutes, shaking the pan.

Tie the lettuce heart with fine string, then add to the pan. Add the sugar and salt and pepper to taste. Pour in enough boiling water to just cover the peas and simmer gently, uncovered, until the peas are tender.

Untie the lettuce heart and stir the leaves into the peas and onions. Serve immediately.

SERVES 6

Courgettes (zucchini), aubergines (eggplant), peppers, tomatoes, green beans and *petits pois* are the vegetables normally associated with French cooking, but cabbages are usually not. And yet in the inland mountainous regions of France, where poor soil and weather force the local people to rely on long-keeping vegetables, the cabbage is an immensely popular vegetable. Hundreds of ingenious ways of cooking cabbage are known to the French that would put our familiar 'boiled greens' to shame!

FARÇON DE CHOU

Cabbage and Bacon Pie

This dish is also sometimes called fouson de chou. In the Savoyarde region there is a similar recipe for gratin de chou in which the cabbage is boiled until tender, then the large outer leaves are stuffed with the inner leaves which have been chopped with bacon. The whole stuffed cabbage is then baked with a little stock in a moderate oven for 2 hours.

Metric/Imperial	American
1 tablespoon olive oil	1 tablespoon olive oil
2 onions, peeled and thinly sliced	2 onions, peeled and thinly sliced
150 g/5 oz smoked streaky bacon, rinds removed and cut into thin strips	$\frac{2}{3}$ cup smoked fatty bacon, cut into thin strips
1 white cabbage, finely shredded	1 white cabbage, finely shredded
2 garlic cloves, peeled and crushed	2 garlic cloves, peeled and crushed
salt	salt
freshly ground black pepper	freshly ground black pepper
2 eggs	2 eggs
150 ml/$\frac{1}{4}$ pint milk	$\frac{2}{3}$ cup milk
2 tablespoons dried breadcrumbs	2 tablespoons dried bread crumbs

Heat the oil in a heavy pan, add the onions and fry gently until golden, stirring occasionally. Add the bacon, cabbage and garlic, and salt and pepper to taste; stir well to mix. (Take care not to add too much salt because of the smoked bacon.) Fry gently for 20 minutes, stirring occasionally.

Whisk the eggs and milk together. Transfer the cabbage mixture to a buttered gratin dish, then pour the egg and milk mixture over the top. Sprinkle with the breadcrumbs and bake in a preheated moderate oven (160°C/325°F/Gas Mark 3) for 1 hour. Serve hot, straight from the gratin dish.
SERVES 6

BOHÉMIENNE

Purée of Aubergines (Eggplant), Tomatoes and Parmesan

A speciality from the town of Avignon, la bohémienne is also sometimes known as gratin estrassaire. It can be eaten hot or cold.

Metric/Imperial	American
1 kg/2 lb aubergines, sliced into thin rounds	2 lb eggplant, sliced into thin rounds
salt	salt
3 tablespoons olive oil	3 tablespoons olive oil
1 onion, peeled and thinly sliced	1 onion, peeled and thinly sliced
4 tomatoes, skinned, chopped and seeded	4 tomatoes, skinned, chopped and seeded
2 garlic cloves, peeled and finely chopped	2 garlic cloves, peeled and finely chopped
chopped parsley	chopped parsley
75 g/3 oz Parmesan cheese, grated	$\frac{3}{4}$ cup grated Parmesan cheese
freshly ground black pepper	freshly ground black pepper

RATATOUILLE NIÇOISE

There are numerous versions of this famous vegetable dish from the Provence region of southern France. This recipe incorporates the usual summer vegetables, but it can equally well be made without some of them – use whatever is available at the time.

Metric/Imperial	American
120 ml/4 fl oz olive oil	$\frac{1}{2}$ cup olive oil
450 g/1 lb aubergines, thinly sliced or diced	1 lb eggplant, thinly sliced or diced
450 g/1 lb courgettes, sliced	1 lb zucchini, sliced
450 g/1 lb onions, peeled and thinly sliced	1 lb onions, peeled and thinly sliced
450 g/1 lb green peppers, cored, seeded and cut into thin strips	1 lb green peppers, cored, seeded and cut into thin strips
5 garlic cloves, peeled and crushed	5 garlic cloves, peeled and crushed
750 g/1$\frac{1}{2}$ lb tomatoes, skinned, halved and seeded	1$\frac{1}{2}$ lb tomatoes, skinned, halved and seeded
salt	salt
freshly ground black pepper	freshly ground black pepper
2 thyme sprigs	2 thyme sprigs
5 large basil leaves	5 large basil leaves
chopped parsley, to garnish	chopped parsley, for garnish

Heat half the oil in a large heavy pan, add the aubergines (eggplant) and fry over moderate heat until lightly coloured, stirring frequently. Add the courgettes (zucchini) and continue frying for 5 to 6 minutes until they are lightly coloured. Remove both aubergines and courgettes with a slotted spoon and set aside.

Add the remaining oil to the pan, then add the onions and fry gently until soft. Add the peppers and garlic, increase the heat and fry for a few minutes. Add the tomatoes and cook gently for 10 minutes, stirring frequently.

Return the aubergines and courgettes to the pan and stir well to mix with the other vegetables. Add salt and pepper to taste, then crumble in the thyme. Cook gently, uncovered, for 40 minutes or until the vegetables are soft, stirring occasionally.

Just before serving, crumble the basil leaves into the ratatouille, then taste and adjust seasoning. Transfer to a warmed serving dish and sprinkle with parsley. Serve hot or cold.

SERVES 6

ABOVE: **Ratatouille niçoise**
LEFT: **Farçon de chou**

Place the aubergine (eggplant) slices in layers in a colander, sprinkling each layer with salt. Leave to dégorge★.

Meanwhile, heat the oil in a large heavy pan, add the onion and fry gently until soft. Add the tomatoes and cook gently, stirring and pressing them firmly to reduce them to a purée.

Drain the aubergines and rinse thoroughly under cold running water. Dry with kitchen paper towels, then add to the pan with the garlic, and parsley to taste. Stir well, then cover and cook gently for 30 minutes. Crush the mixture with a wooden spoon from time to time to mash the aubergines to a purée.

A few minutes before the end of cooking, stir in the Parmesan, then taste and adjust seasoning. Transfer to a warmed serving dish and serve hot.

SERVES 6

VARIATION: Some versions of *la bohémienne* contain anchovies: Desalt★ canned anchovy fillets, then cook them in a little olive oil, stirring with a wooden spoon until they are reduced to a purée. Mix with a little milk, then with the Parmesan, and spread over the top of the aubergine purée in a gratin dish. Bake in a preheated hot oven (220°C/425°F/Gas Mark 7) for 10 minutes or until golden brown. Serve hot, straight from the gratin dish.

FABONADE

Broad (Lima) Beans with Ham and Garlic in Creamy Sauce

Metric/Imperial
50 g/2 oz saindoux★,
   dripping or butter
1 onion, peeled and finely
   chopped
150 g/5 oz ham★, diced
4 garlic cloves, peeled and
   crushed
1 kg/2 lb broad beans,
   shelled
150 ml/¼ pint water
few savory sprigs
salt
freshly ground black pepper
4 egg yolks
2 teaspoons wine vinegar or
   lemon juice
chopped parsley, to garnish

American
¼ cup saindoux★, drippings
   or butter
1 onion, peeled and finely
   chopped
⅔ cup diced ham★
4 garlic cloves, peeled and
   crushed
2 lb lima beans, shelled
⅔ cup water
few savory sprigs
salt
freshly ground black pepper
4 egg yolks
2 tablespoons wine vinegar
   or lemon juice
chopped parsley, for garnish

Melt the fat in a heavy pan, add the onion and ham and fry gently for a few minutes. Add the garlic and beans, then the water, savory, and salt and pepper to taste. Mix well.

Bring to the boil, then lower the heat, cover and simmer for 20 to 30 minutes until the beans are tender.

Discard the savory. Mix the egg yolks and vinegar or lemon juice together, then stir slowly into the beans. Heat through, but do not allow to boil. Taste and adjust seasoning, then transfer to a warmed serving dish and garnish with parsley. Serve immediately.
SERVES 6

CHOU ROUGE AUX POMMES

Braised Red Cabbage with Apples

Metric/Imperial
25 g/1 oz goose fat★,
   dripping or butter
1 large onion, peeled and
   sliced
1 red cabbage, coarsely
   shredded
salt
freshly ground black pepper
200 ml/8 fl oz chicken stock
   (page 8)
pinch of sugar
1 bay leaf
1 whole clove
3 cooking apples, peeled,
   cored and thinly sliced

American
2 tablespoons goose fat★,
   drippings or butter
1 large onion, peeled and
   sliced
1 red cabbage, coarsely
   shredded
salt
freshly ground black pepper
1 cup chicken stock
   (page 8)
pinch of sugar
1 bay leaf
1 whole clove
3 tart apples, peeled, cored
   and thinly sliced

Melt the fat in a large flameproof casserole, add the onion and fry gently until soft but not coloured. Add the cabbage with salt and pepper to taste, then moisten with half of the stock. Stir in the sugar, bay leaf and clove, then cover and cook very gently for 45 minutes.

Add the apples to the casserole, folding them in gently to mix with the cabbage. Cover again and cook for a further 45 minutes or until the cabbage and apples are tender. Add the remaining stock a little at a time during cooking as the cabbage becomes dry.

Discard the bay leaf and clove, then taste and adjust seasoning. Serve hot, straight from the casserole.
SERVES 4 TO 5

Fabonade; Tian de légumes

The word *tian* is Provençal dialect, for which there is no direct translation. It is used to describe a kind of gratin dish, both the vessel in which the food is cooked and the food itself. A *tian* is usually a mixture of vegetables and eggs topped with grated cheese and breadcrumbs; spinach is probably the best-known *tian* but it is equally delicious made with courgettes (zucchini) or a mixture of different vegetables.

TIAN DE LÉGUMES

Spinach au Gratin

Metric/Imperial	American
4 tablespoons olive oil	*¼ cup olive oil*
1.5 kg/3–3½ lb spinach, thinly sliced	*3–3½ lb spinach, thinly sliced*
2 garlic cloves, peeled and bruised	*2 garlic cloves, peeled and bruised*
salt	*salt*
freshly ground black pepper	*freshly ground black pepper*
1 egg, beaten	*1 egg, beaten*
50 g/2 oz fresh breadcrumbs	*1 cup fresh bread crumbs*
50 g/2 oz Gruyère cheese★, grated	*½ cup grated Gruyère cheese★*

Heat half the oil in a large heavy pan. Add the spinach with just the water clinging to the leaves after washing, the garlic and a little salt and pepper. Cook, uncovered, over brisk heat for 10 minutes until all the water from the spinach has evaporated.

Discard the garlic, then leave the spinach to cool slightly. Stir in the beaten egg, reheat gently, then taste and adjust seasoning.

Transfer the spinach to an oiled gratin dish and level the surface. Mix together the breadcrumbs and cheese, sprinkle over the top, then sprinkle with the remaining oil. Put under a preheated hot grill (broiler) for 5 minutes or until the topping is golden brown. Serve hot.
SERVES 6

Tian aux oeufs: Make as above, adding a layer of 6 sliced hard-boiled eggs in the middle of the spinach.
Tian de courgettes (zucchini): Make as above, but use 1 kg/2 lb courgettes (zucchini) instead of the spinach. Cut the courgettes diagonally into 5 mm/¼ inch thick slices and cook for 10 minutes as for spinach.

GRATIN DAUPHINOIS

Layered Potatoes with Cream and Garlic

Metric/Imperial	American
1 garlic clove, peeled	1 garlic clove, peeled
75 g/3 oz butter	$\frac{1}{3}$ cup butter
1 kg/2 lb waxy potatoes, peeled and sliced into thin rounds	2 lb waxy potatoes, peeled and sliced into thin rounds
freshly grated nutmeg	freshly grated nutmeg
salt	salt
freshly ground black pepper	freshly ground black pepper
about 250 ml/8 fl oz hot milk	about 1 cup hot milk
about 250 ml/8 fl oz single cream	about 1 cup light cream

Rub the inside of an earthenware or enamel baking dish with the garlic, then brush thickly with butter.

Place the potato slices in the dish in layers, sprinkling each layer with nutmeg, salt and pepper to taste.

Mix the milk and cream together, then pour over the potatoes, making sure the potatoes are completely covered with the liquid. Dot the top with the remaining butter.

Bake uncovered, in a preheated moderate oven (180°C/350°F/Gas Mark 4) for 1 to 1¼ hours until the potatoes are tender when pierced with a skewer. Increase the heat to moderately hot (200°C/400°F/Gas Mark 6) for the last 10 minutes' cooking time to brown the top layer of potatoes. Serve hot, straight from the baking dish.

SERVES 4 TO 6

LENTILLES DU PUY

Lentils Auvergne-Style

Lentils from Le Puy in the Auvergne are the small dark green variety, not to be confused with other brown, red or yellow lentils. Lentilles du Puy can be bought in good French delicatessens. They are sold ready to cook, with grit removed, but before cooking, wash them in a bowl of warm water and discard any that float to the surface.

Metric/Imperial	American
450 g/1 lb green lentils	2 cups green lentils
2 litres/3½ pints water	4½ pints (9 cups) water
salt	salt
freshly ground black pepper	freshly ground black pepper
100 g/4 oz belly pork	¼ lb pork sides
2 onions, peeled	2 onions, peeled
2 whole cloves	2 whole cloves
2 carrots, peeled and halved lengthways	2 carrots, peeled and halved lengthways
1 celery stick	1 celery stick
1 bouquet garni★	1 bouquet garni★
1 tablespoon saindoux★, dripping or butter	1 tablespoon saindoux★, drippings or butter
2 garlic cloves, peeled and thinly sliced	2 garlic cloves, peeled and thinly sliced
2 tablespoons plain flour	2 tablespoons flour
300 ml/½ pint vegetable stock (page 9)	1¼ cups vegetable stock (page 9)

French potato dishes are
often flavoured with
nutmeg. Never use the
ready-ground nutmeg
sold in drums or jars;
follow the French
tradition – buy whole
nutmegs and grate them
on the fine side of a
conical or box cheese
grater. Better still, buy a
special nutmeg grater or
grinder to encourage you
to grate nutmeg freshly
as and when required.
The difference in flavour
between ground and
freshly grated nutmeg is
incomparable.

Soak the lentils in cold water for 1 hour. Drain and place in a large pan. Add boiling water to cover and simmer just below boiling point for 5 minutes. Drain.

Bring the measured water to the boil in the rinsed-out pan. Add salt and pepper to taste, the pork, 1 onion stuck with the cloves, the carrots, celery and bouquet garni. Bring back to the boil, then add the lentils. Simmer, covered, for 1¼ hours or until the lentils and pork are tender.

Meanwhile, melt the fat in a flameproof casserole, slice the remaining onion, then add to the fat with the garlic. Fry gently until golden, then sprinkle in the flour. Cook, stirring, for 1 minute to obtain a smooth *roux* (paste). Stir in the stock gradually, then bring slowly to the boil, stirring. Lower the heat and simmer for 5 to 6 minutes, stirring frequently.

Drain the lentils and discard the whole onion, cloves, carrots, celery and bouquet garni. Dice the pork. Stir the lentils and pork into the sauce and heat through gently. Taste and adjust seasoning, then transfer to a warmed serving dish. Serve hot.

SERVES 6

TRUFFIAT

Potato Cake

Metric/Imperial	American
1 kg/2 lb floury old potatoes, peeled	2 lb floury old potatoes, peeled
3 eggs, beaten	3 eggs, beaten
150 g/5 oz butter, softened	⅔ cup softened butter
freshly grated nutmeg	freshly grated nutmeg
salt	salt
freshly ground black pepper	freshly ground black pepper
250 g/9 oz plain flour	2¼ cups all-purpose flour

Steam the potatoes, in a pressure-cooker if possible, or cook in a small amount of water until just tender, to avoid them becoming too moist. Mash or purée them in an electric blender or *mouli-légumes* (vegetable mill). Beat in the eggs (reserving a little for the glaze), then 50 g/2 oz/¼ cup butter and nutmeg, salt and pepper to taste.

Mix the flour and the remaining butter together with a little water to form a soft dough. Mix the potato purée with the dough, then knead until smooth.

Form the potato dough into a rectangular shape about 2 cm/¾ inch thick in a buttered baking dish. Make criss-cross incisions in the top, then brush with the reserved beaten egg.

Bake in a preheated moderate oven (180°C/350°F/Gas Mark 4) for about 45 minutes or until the top is golden brown. The inside of the cake should still be quite moist. Serve hot, straight from the baking dish.

SERVES 6

VARIATION: A little grated cheese can be added to the dough while mixing.

Rather than mixing the two doughs together, the flour dough can be formed into a rectangular shape and placed in the baking dish, then the potato purée spread on top.

DESSERTS

The French prefer cheese and fresh fruit to desserts, the cheese being served after the main course to finish up the last of the wine, and the fruit after the cheese to cleanse the palate. Sometimes, especially in summer, the fruit comes in the form of a chilled compote, a simple dish of fresh fruit poached with sugar and water or wine, occasionally with a dash of brandy or liqueur added. In winter, dried fruits are sometimes poached and served warm. Poached fruit bears little or no resemblance to its stewed counterpart so frequently served in Britain — the fruit is cooked very gently so that it retains its shape and texture.

If you are serving a meal in the French style, with an hors d'oeuvre or soup followed by a main dish of meat, poultry or fish, a separate vegetable dish, then a French cheese or two, you will quickly find that a rich, creamy dessert is almost impossible to eat! For everyday meals, the French housewife occasionally makes a light creamy dessert, a milk-based pudding or a crème caramel (page 86), especially if there are children, but in most cases there will only be a fruit yogurt or a soft creamy cheese such as a petit-suisse sprinkled with sugar or topped with some poached fruit. The dessert course only really comes into its own at dinner parties and on special occasions, when fruit-filled crêpes, a crème brûlée or a sweet soufflé might be served. Fresh fruit tarts with crème patissière are also popular, but in many cases when a French housewife is entertaining, she will send out to the local pâtisserie for her pastries, tarts and gâteaux.

Every French town, however small, sports its own pâtisserie, and the visitor to France cannot help but notice the sumptuous array of tarts, pastries, gâteaux and sweetmeats that are displayed in the window. In France it is just as acceptable to offer your guests a tart bought from the pâtissier, as it is to serve a home-made one, for the quality is at least comparable. Unfortunately fine pâtisserie is not so easy to find in this country and elaborate desserts are best prepared at home.

CRÊPES SUZETTE

Orange-flavoured liqueur and the zest and juice of oranges is the traditional flavouring for this classic dish, but some people may prefer the more unusual flavour of mandarins — the choice is up to you!

Metric/Imperial	**American**
BATTER:	BATTER:
125 g/4½ oz plain flour	1 cup plus 2 tablespoons all-purpose flour
¼ teaspoon salt	¼ teaspoon salt
3 eggs	3 eggs
2 tablespoons oil	2 tablespoons oil
50 g/2 oz butter, melted	¼ cup melted butter
1 tablespoon caster sugar	1 tablespoon sugar
2 teaspoons vanilla sugar★	2 teaspoons vanilla sugar★
350 ml/12 fl oz milk	1½ cups milk
1 tablespoon rum	1 tablespoon rum
25 g/1 oz butter, for frying	2 tablespoons butter, for frying
SYRUP:	SYRUP:
100 g/4 oz butter, softened and diced	½ cup softened butter, diced
100 g/4 oz caster sugar	½ cup sugar
6 tablespoons Cointreau or Grand Marnier	6 tablespoons Cointreau or Grand Marnier
3 tablespoons brandy	3 tablespoons brandy
1 orange or 2 mandarins	1 orange or 2 mandarins

For the batter, sift the flour and salt into a bowl and make a well in the centre. Add the remaining batter ingredients, then beat well to mix until smooth, using an electric mixer if available. Pass the batter through a fine sieve (strainer) to remove any lumps.

CRÊPES BRETONNES
Apple Crêpes

In Brittany these crêpes are often served as a dessert with jam, honey, chocolate sauce or fruit in syrup.

Metric/Imperial	American
250 g/9 oz wholewheat flour	2¼ cups wholewheat flour
4 eggs	4 eggs
2 tablespoons oil	2 tablespoons oil
5 tablespoons caster sugar	5 tablespoons sugar
150 g/5 oz butter	⅔ cup butter
250 ml/8 fl oz warm milk	1 cup warm milk
1 teaspoon orange flower water★	1 teaspoon orange flower water★
450 g/1 lb eating apples, peeled, cored and thinly sliced	1 lb dessert apples, peeled, cored and thinly sliced

Put the flour in a bowl and make a well in the centre. Add the eggs, oil and sugar, then beat until smooth, using an electric mixer if available.

Melt 50 g/2 oz/¼ cup butter in the warm milk, then whisk into the batter with a fork until thoroughly incorporated. Pass the batter through a fine sieve (strainer) to remove any lumps, then whisk in the orange flower water. If the batter seems too thick, add a little cold water until a thin, pouring consistency is obtained.

Melt 50 g/2 oz/¼ cup butter in a heavy pan, add the apple slices and fry gently until golden. Keep hot in the pan.

Melt the remaining butter in a 20 cm/8 inch crêpe pan or frying pan (skillet). Pour off the butter into a warmed jug.

Pour a small ladleful of batter into the pan, then tilt the pan from the side to side so that the batter runs and covers the base of the pan evenly. Sprinkle a few apple slices over the crêpe, then fry over brisk heat for 10 to 15 seconds until golden brown on the underside. Turn or toss the crêpe over and fry the other side for 10 to 15 seconds until golden brown. Keep hot while frying the remaining batter and apples, pouring a little melted butter into the pan in between making the crêpes, as the pan becomes dry. Serve hot.

SERVES 8

Crêpes suzette

Melt the butter for frying in a 20 cm/8 inch crêpe pan or frying pan (skillet). Pour off the butter into a warmed jug.

Pour a small ladleful of batter into the pan, then tilt the pan from side to side so that the batter runs and covers the base of the pan evenly. Fry over brisk heat for 10 to 15 seconds until golden brown on the underside, then turn or toss the crêpe over and fry the other side for 10 to 15 seconds until golden brown.

Slide the crêpe onto a warmed platter and keep hot while frying the remainder. Pour a little melted butter into the pan in between making the crêpes as the pan becomes dry.

Ten minutes before serving, make the syrup. Put the butter in the pan in which the crêpes were cooked. Add the sugar, 2 tablespoons liqueur and 1 tablespoon brandy. Grate the zest★ of the orange or mandarins finely into the pan, then squeeze in the juice from the fruit.

Place the pan over brisk heat and boil rapidly for 1 minute until a thick syrup is obtained. Lower the heat and leave to simmer.

Add the crêpes to the pan one at a time to coat them in the syrup, fold each one in half, then in half again to make a triangular shape. Place on a warmed serving platter and keep hot by standing the platter over a pan of gently simmering water. Repeat with the remaining crêpes, pouring any remaining syrup over the finished crêpes.

Warm the remaining liqueur and brandy in a separate small pan. Set light to the liqueur in the pan, then pour over the crêpes at the table. Serve as soon as the flames have died down.

SERVES 6 to 8

CRÈME CARAMEL

A classic French dessert with many variations.

Metric/Imperial	American
CUSTARD:	CUSTARD:
1 litre/1¾ pints milk	4¼ cups milk
1 vanilla pod★, split in half lengthways	1 vanilla bean★, split in half lengthways
8 eggs	8 eggs
100 g/4 oz sugar	½ cup sugar
CARAMEL:	CARAMEL:
100 g/4 oz sugar	½ cup sugar
2 tablespoons water	2 tablespoons water
1 teaspoon lemon juice	1 teaspoon lemon juice

Put the milk in a heavy pan with the vanilla and bring slowly to the boil. Remove from the heat and leave to infuse.

Meanwhile, make the caramel: put the sugar, water and lemon juice in a small heavy pan. Cook over moderate heat until a rich golden caramel colour is obtained. Remove from the heat and pour immediately into a warmed 2 litre/3½ pint/9 cup charlotte or ring mould, soufflé dish or *moule à manqué*. Rotate the mould or dish quickly so that the caramel coats the base and sides evenly. Set aside.

Make the custard: whisk the eggs and sugar together in a bowl until thoroughly combined. Discard the vanilla from the infused milk, then whisk the milk into the egg and sugar mixture. Pass the mixture through a fine sieve (strainer) into the caramelized mould.

Stand the mould in a hot *bain marie* and place in a preheated moderate oven (180°C/350°F/Gas Mark 4). Immediately lower the temperature to cool (150°C/300°F/Gas Mark 2). Cook for about 1 hour or until set; to test if the custard is set, insert a knife into the centre – it should be clean when withdrawn.

Remove the *crème caramel* from the *bain marie* and leave until cold. Leave in a cool place or chill in the refrigerator for 4 hours before unmoulding onto a deep serving dish. To unmould easily, dip the base of the mould into a bowl of hot water for 30 seconds.

Serve *crème caramel* at room temperature or chilled, according to taste.
SERVES 8

VARIATIONS:

1. *Crème caramel* can be baked in 8 individual ramekins or soufflé dishes if preferred, in which case the cooking time should only be 45 minutes.
2. If a more solid custard is preferred, use 4 whole eggs and 8 egg yolks instead of the 8 whole eggs suggested above.
3. The milk can be infused with orange or lemon zest★ as well as, or instead of, the vanilla.
4. The custard can be baked on its own without the caramel, in which case it is called *oeufs au lait*. Brush the mould lightly with butter before pouring in the custard – without the caramel it is likely to stick. If liked, a caramel sauce can be made separately and poured over the custard before serving. Make the caramel sauce by cooking 150 g/5 oz/⅔ cup sugar with 7 tablespoons water until a golden caramel liquid is obtained.

5. If baking the custard on its own without the caramel sauce, the custard itself can be flavoured with chocolate or coffee. Whisk 50 g/2 oz/½ cup cocoa powder or 2 tablespoons instant coffee powder into the eggs and sugar. Increase the quantity of sugar in the custard to 50 g/2 oz/¼ cup.

CLAFOUTIS
Cherry Custard Pudding

It is traditional to remove the stalks from the cherries, but not to stone (pit) them. The size of the baking dish is important when making clafoutis – it should be shallow, but large enough to contain all the cherries in a single layer so that the custard sets evenly around the fruit. Do not use a deep dish in which the cherries have to be piled on top of each other.

Metric/Imperial	American
50 g/2 oz butter, softened	¼ cup softened butter
750 g/1½ lb ripe black cherries	1½ lb ripe black cherries
2 eggs	2 eggs
1 egg yolk	1 egg yolk
100 g/4 oz caster sugar	½ cup sugar
pinch of salt	pinch of salt
50 g/2 oz plain flour	½ cup all-purpose flour
250 ml/8 fl oz milk	1 cup milk
2 teaspoons vanilla sugar★	2 teaspoons vanilla sugar★

Brush the inside of a large shallow baking dish or mould with a little of the softened butter. Arrange the cherries in the bottom of the dish side by side, keeping them in a single layer.

Put the whole eggs and egg yolk in a bowl, add the sugar and salt, then whisk together until light and fluffy.

Melt the remaining butter and whisk into the egg mixture. Whisk in the flour, then add the milk and continue whisking until the batter is smooth.

Pour the batter over the cherries, then bake uncovered in a preheated moderately hot oven (190°C/375°F/Gas Mark 5) for 40 minutes, or until the *clafoutis* is puffed and golden brown. Remove from the oven and leave to cool slightly, until warm.

Sprinkle with the vanilla sugar just before serving. Serve warm, straight from the baking dish.
SERVES 6

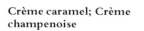

Crème caramel; Crème champenoise

CRÈME CHAMPENOISE

White Wine and Lemon Cream

If possible, use a still white wine from the Champagne region (not champagne) for this light, creamy dessert.

Metric/Imperial	American
6 eggs, separated	6 eggs, separated
2 tablespoons cornflour	2 tablespoons cornstarch
grated rind and juice of 1 lemon	grated rind and juice of 1 lemon
100 g/4 oz caster sugar	½ cup sugar
350 ml/12 fl oz dry white wine	1½ cups dry white wine

Place 2 egg yolks and the cornflour in a bowl and beat until smooth. Add the remaining egg yolks, lemon rind and juice, and 2 tablespoons of the sugar; beat thoroughly. Heat the wine in a pan to just below boiling, then gradually stir in the egg yolk mixture.

Stand the bowl over a pan of hot water and continue whisking until the mixture is thick and creamy. Remove the bowl from the heat and continue whisking until cool.

Whisk the egg whites in a separate bowl until stiff, then whisk in the sugar a little at a time. Fold 2 tablespoons of the egg white mixture into the custard, then carefully fold in the remaining mixture. Turn into a serving bowl. Chill in the refrigerator for up to 1 hour. Serve with thin crisp biscuits (cookies).
SERVES 8

CRÉMETS D'ANGERS

Whipped Cream Dessert

Sometimes the simplest dishes are the most delicious and crémets is no exception, served with fresh strawberries or raspberries, or simply with sugar and cream.
In France, crémets are made in special porcelain or metal moulds, which have holes in the base to allow for drainage. Although the moulds can be bought outside France, you can improvise and make your own by punching holes in a small plastic container. Remember to stand the mould over a dish to catch the drips from the cream.

Metric/Imperial	American
120 ml/4 fl oz double cream, chilled	½ cup heavy cream, chilled
1 egg white	1 egg white
sugar and cream, to serve	sugar and cream, to serve

Whip the cream until stiff. Beat the egg white in a separate bowl until stiff, then fold into the cream until thoroughly incorporated.

Turn the mixture into a muslin (cheesecloth) lined mould, then cover and place in the refrigerator. Leave to drain for 3 to 6 hours.

Turn the *crémets* onto a serving dish and serve immediately, with sugar and cream.
SERVES 2

SOUFFLÉ GLACÉ AUX MIRABELLES

Iced Plum Soufflé

Alsace-Lorraine is famous for its small garden plums known as mirabelles, which are perfect for this recipe. If they are not available, other varieties can be used. Mirabelles are used extensively in the cooking of this region; they are also made into a liqueur known as eau-de-vie de mirabelles. In this recipe the liqueur gives the finished soufflé a heady plum flavour, but if it is difficult to obtain, use kirsch instead.

Metric/Imperial

500 g/1 lb fresh plums, halved and stoned
300 ml/½ pint double cream, chilled
2 tablespoons eau-de-vie de mirabelles or kirsch
4 egg whites
175 g/6 oz caster sugar
TO DECORATE:
about 25 g/1 oz finely chopped nuts or crushed ratafias
about 120 ml/4 fl oz double or whipping cream, whipped

American

1 lb fresh plums, halved and pitted
1¼ cups heavy cream, chilled
2 tablespoons eau-de-vie de mirabelles or kirsch
4 egg whites
¾ cup sugar
TO DECORATE:
about ¼ cup finely chopped nuts or crushed ratafias
about ½ cup heavy or whipping cream, whipped

Prepare a 1.2 litre/2 pint/5 cup freezerproof soufflé dish: cut a strip of doubled greaseproof (waxed) paper long enough to go around the outside of the dish and stand 5 cm/2 inches higher. Tie this securely around the outside of the dish and brush the inside above the rim with melted butter.

Work the fruit in an electric blender or *mouli-légumes* (vegetable mill), then sieve (strain) to remove the skins. Whip the cream until it just holds its shape, then fold into the fruit purée until thoroughly incorporated. Whisk in the liqueur. Set aside.

Beat the egg whites in a separate bowl until stiff and standing in peaks, then add the sugar a little at a time, beating constantly after each addition until thoroughly incorporated.

Fold the egg whites into the fruit purée mixture a little at a time. Do not whisk the mixture as this will knock the air out of the egg whites and cause the soufflé to lose body and lightness.

Spoon the mixture into the prepared soufflé dish, then freeze for at least 4 hours until firm. Thirty minutes before serving, carefully peel off the greaseproof paper and place the soufflé in the refrigerator to soften.

Press nuts or ratafias around the edge and decorate the top with piped whipped cream before serving.
SERVES 6 to 8

ABRICOTS À L'ALSACIENNE

Apricots Baked with Sugar and Kirsch

Metric/Imperial	American
750 g/1½ lb ripe fresh apricots, halved and stoned	1½ lb ripe fresh apricots, halved and pitted
4 tablespoons water	¼ cup water
150 g/5 oz sugar	⅔ cup sugar
2 tablespoons kirsch	2 tablespoons kirsch

Put the apricots, cut side down, in a baking dish. Mix the water and half the sugar together, then pour over the apricots.

Bake in a preheated moderately hot oven (200°C/400°F/Gas Mark 6) for about 30 minutes until the apricots are tender.

Pour the kirsch into the bottom of the dish, then sprinkle the apricots with the remaining sugar. Put under a preheated hot grill (broiler) as close to the flame as possible, then grill (broil) for a few minutes until browned. Serve hot or cold, straight from the baking dish.

SERVES 6

Charlotte aux framboises; Soufflé glacé aux mirabelles

CHARLOTTE AUX FRAMBOISES

Raspberry Cream Charlotte

If liked, serve this spectacular-looking dessert with crème anglaise (page 16)

Metric/Imperial	American
4 egg yolks	4 egg yolks
100 g/4 oz caster sugar	½ cup sugar
250 ml/8 fl oz boiling hot milk	1 cup boiling hot milk
15 g/½ oz gelatine	2 envelopes gelatin
120 ml/4 fl oz cold water	½ cup cold water
150 ml/¼ pint double cream, chilled	⅔ cup heavy cream, chilled
about 2 teaspoons vanilla sugar★	about 2 teaspoons vanilla sugar★
350 g/12 oz fresh raspberries, hulled	2½ cups hulled fresh raspberries
4 tablespoons kirsch	¼ cup kirsch
about 28 (2 packets) sponge fingers	about 28 ladyfingers
TO DECORATE:	TO DECORATE:
about 150 ml/¼ pint double cream, whipped	about ⅔ cup heavy cream, whipped
100 g/4 oz fresh raspberries	1 cup fresh raspberries

Whisk the egg yolks and sugar together in a heatproof bowl until thick and pale. Pour in the milk a little at a time, stirring constantly with a wooden spoon. Stand the bowl over a pan of gently simmering water and cook gently, stirring, until the custard coats the back of the spoon; this may take up to 20 minutes.

Meanwhile, sprinkle the gelatine over 4 tablespoons/¼ cup of the water in a small heatproof bowl and leave to soak for a few minutes. Stand the bowl in a pan of hot water until the gelatine has dissolved, stirring if necessary. Remove the thickened custard from the heat and stir in the dissolved gelatine. Leave until cold.

Whip the cream until it just holds its shape, then whip in the vanilla sugar. Fold into the cold custard with the raspberries and half of the kirsch.

Pour the remaining kirsch and water into a shallow dish. Dip the sponge fingers (ladyfingers) one at a time into the liquid, then use to line the base and sides of a lightly oiled 15 to 18 cm/6 to 7 inch charlotte mould or soufflé dish, reserving a few for the top. Stand the biscuits upright, sugared side outwards, as close together as possible and trimming them to fit if necessary.

Fill the centre of the mould with the raspberry cream mixture, level the top, then cover with the reserved sponge fingers. Chill in the refrigerator for at least 3 hours until the filling is set.

To serve, unmould the charlotte onto a chilled serving platter. Decorate with the whipped cream and raspberries. Serve chilled.

SERVES 6 to 8

VACHERIN
Strawberry Meringue Gâteau

In France, the meringue base and shells for vacherin can be bought ready made at most pâtisseries.

Metric/Imperial	American
MERINGUE:	MERINGUE:
3 egg whites	3 egg whites
75 g/3 oz icing sugar, sifted	¾ cup sifted confectioner's sugar
75 g/3 oz caster sugar	⅓ cup sugar
TO FINISH:	TO FINISH:
250 ml/8 fl oz crème chantilly (page 16)	1 cup crème chantilly (page 16)
100 g/4 oz sugar	½ cup sugar
7 tablespoons water	7 tablespoons water
450 g/1 lb fresh strawberries	3 cups fresh strawberries
about 500 ml/18 fl oz vanilla ice cream	about 2¼ cups vanilla ice cream
about 500 ml/18 fl oz strawberry ice cream	about 2¼ cups strawberry ice cream

Make the meringue: beat the egg whites until stiff and standing in peaks, then fold in the sugars gradually until thoroughly incorporated.

Place a sheet of non-stick parchment paper on a baking sheet. Draw an 18 cm/7 inch circle on the paper, then spread with half of the meringue mixture.

Put the remaining meringue into a piping bag fitted with a 2.5 cm/1 inch fluted nozzle. On a separate sheet of parchment paper, pipe the remaining meringue into shell shapes, about 5 cm/2 inches long. Bake the circle and the shells in a preheated cool oven (140°C/275°F/Gas Mark 1) for 1 hour or until the meringue is firm and dry but still white. Leave until cold before peeling off the paper.

Place the meringue circle on a serving platter. Sandwich the shells together in pairs with a little of the *crème chantilly*, then stick around the edge of the circle with more *crème chantilly*.

Put the sugar and water in a heavy pan and heat gently until the sugar has dissolved. Bring to the boil and boil rapidly until thick and syrupy. Remove from the heat and leave to cool.

Reserve 12 whole strawberries for the decoration, then work the remaining strawberries through the fine blade of a *mouli-légumes* (vegetable mill) or purée in an electric blender. Stir in the sugar syrup to make a strawberry sauce or *coulis*.

Scoop the ice cream into the centre of the *vacherin* and dot with some of the reserved whole strawberries. Pour over about one third of the strawberry sauce, then decorate with the remaining whole strawberries and the remaining *crème chantilly*. Serve immediately, with the remaining strawberry sauce handed separately in a sauceboat.
SERVES 6

TARTE AUX POMMES
Creamy Apple Flan

In Alsace-Lorraine this flan is often given the name 'chaude'. Sometimes the custard topping is flavoured with a local eau-de-vie, cinnamon or vanilla, then the flan takes the name of 'migaine'.

Metric/Imperial	American
PÂTE SABLÉE:	PÂTE SABLÉE:
250 g/9 oz plain flour	2¼ cups all-purpose flour
pinch of salt	pinch of salt
125 g/4½ oz butter, cut into small pieces	½ cup plus 1 tablespoon butter, cut into small pieces
1 egg yolk	1 egg yolk
50 g/2 oz caster sugar	¼ cup sugar
3–4 tablespoons iced water	3–4 tablespoons iced water
FILLING:	FILLING:
juice of 1 lemon	juice of 1 lemon
750 g/1½ lb crisp eating apples	1½ lb crisp dessert apples
75 ml/3 fl oz milk	⅓ cup milk
75 ml/3 fl oz double cream	⅓ cup heavy cream
2 eggs, beaten	2 eggs, beaten
50 g/2 oz caster sugar	¼ cup sugar

To make the *pâte sablée*, sift the flour and salt into a bowl and make a well in the centre. Add the butter, egg yolk and sugar, then work the ingredients together with the fingertips, adding the water gradually until a smooth, soft dough is obtained. Leave in the refrigerator for at least 1 hour.

Roll out the dough on a floured surface and use to line the base and sides of a buttered 25 cm/10 inch flan dish or tart pan (preferably with a removable base). Set aside.

For the filling, pour the lemon juice into a large bowl. Peel, quarter and core the apples one at a time, then slice thinly into the bowl of lemon juice, stirring to prevent discoloration.

Arrange the apple slices in the flan dish in a circular pattern, working from the edge of the dish inwards, and overlapping the slices slightly. Stand the dish on a baking sheet and bake in a preheated hot oven (230°C/450°F/Gas Mark 8) for 10 minutes.

Meanwhile, put the remaining filling ingredients in a bowl and whisk together. Pour over the apples in the flan dish and bake in a moderately hot oven (200°C/400°F/Gas Mark 6) for a further 30 minutes. Leave to cool slightly, then serve straight from the dish or transfer to a serving platter. Serve warm.
SERVES 8

Alsace-Lorraine is the real home of *tartes* and *quiches*, both sweet and savoury. The basic filling for both of these is egg custard, the difference is simply that fruit and sugar are added for a sweet flan, whereas cheese, onion and bacon are more usual for a savoury filling. Fruit orchards are as prolific in the region as *quiches*, and all kinds of fruit are used to make creamy *tartes*, including cherries, apricots and bilberries, as well as apples.

DOUILLONS
Baked Apple Parcels

Douillons are often made with whole pears instead of apples as in this recipe, and sometimes the shortcrust pastry (pie dough) is replaced by pâte feuilletée (puff pastry).

Metric/Imperial	American
PÂTE SABLÉE:	PÂTE SABLÉE:
250 g/9 oz plain flour	2¼ cups all-purpose flour
pinch of salt	pinch of salt
125 g/4½ oz butter, cut into small pieces	½ cup plus 1 tablespoon butter, cut into small pieces
1 egg yolk	1 egg yolk
25 g/1 oz caster sugar	2 tablespoons sugar
a little iced water, to mix	a little iced water, to mix
APPLE FILLING:	APPLE FILLING:
50 g/2 oz caster sugar	¼ cup sugar
50 g/2 oz butter, softened	¼ cup softened butter
1 teaspoon ground cinnamon	1 teaspoon ground cinnamon
4 large eating apples	4 large dessert apples
juice of 1 lemon	juice of 1 lemon
GLAZE:	GLAZE:
1 egg	1 egg
1 tablespoon water	1 tablespoon water

To make the *pâte sablée*, sift the flour and salt into a bowl and make a well in the centre. Add the butter, egg yolk and sugar, then work the ingredients together with the fingertips, adding the water gradually until a smooth, soft dough is obtained. Leave in the refrigerator for at least 1 hour.

Meanwhile, make the apple filling. Mix together the sugar, butter and cinnamon. Peel and core the apples, making enough room in the centre of each one for the butter and sugar mixture. Sprinkle the apples immediately with the lemon juice to prevent discoloration.

Roll out the dough on a floured surface until very thin, then cut into 4 equal squares. Place 1 apple in the centre of each square, then divide the butter and sugar mixture equally between them, pushing it well down into the central cavity. If there is any mixture left over, spread it over the top of the apples.

Wrap the dough around the apples to enclose them completely, then moisten the edges with water and press together to seal. Stand the parcels on a dampened baking sheet and decorate with leaves cut from the pastry trimmings. Beat together the egg and water for the glaze and brush all over the dough.

Bake in a preheated moderately hot oven (200°C/400°F/Gas Mark 6) for 30 minutes. Serve hot or cold.
SERVES 4

Tarte aux pommes;
Douillons

TARTE TATIN

Upside-Down Apple Tart

This tart is named after the young ladies Tatin, who owned a restaurant in Sologne at the beginning of this century called 'Le Motte-Beuvron'.

Metric/Imperial	American
100 g/4 oz butter, softened	$\frac{1}{2}$ cup softened butter
100 g/4 oz caster sugar	$\frac{1}{2}$ cup sugar
1.5 kg/2$\frac{1}{2}$ lb small crisp dessert apples	2$\frac{1}{2}$ lb small crisp dessert apples
225 g/8 oz pâte brisée (page 18)	$\frac{1}{2}$ lb pâté brisée (page 18)

Brush the base of a 23 to 25 cm/9 to 10 inch round flameproof baking dish with two thirds of the butter. Sprinkle with two thirds of the sugar.

Peel, halve and core the apples. Arrange the apple halves in the dish, cut sides facing upwards and pressing them firmly together. (It does not matter if they come above the edge of the dish – they will shrink down during cooking.) Sprinkle with the remaining sugar, then dot with the remaining butter.

Cook the apples over moderate heat for about 20 minutes until they begin to caramelize underneath. Transfer to a preheated moderately hot oven (200°C/400°F/Gas Mark 6) and bake for about 5 minutes until the apples become caramelized on top. Remove from the oven and set aside.

Roll out the pastry (dough) thinly on a floured surface to a circle large enough to cover the baking dish. Place the pastry over the dish, then trim around the edge with a knife so that the pastry falls inside the dish to enclose the apples.

Return the dish to the hot oven and bake for a further 20 minutes or until the pastry is crisp and golden. Remove from the oven and immediately invert the dish onto a serving platter. Leave to cool slightly. Serve warm.

SERVES 6

POIRAT DU BERRY

Pear Tart with Brandy and Cream

Metric/Imperial	American
1 kg/2 lb firm cooking pears	2 lb firm cooking pears
4 tablespoons brandy	$\frac{1}{4}$ cup brandy
100 g/4 oz caster sugar	$\frac{1}{2}$ cup sugar
pinch of pepper	pinch of pepper
350 g/12 oz pâte brisée (page 18)	$\frac{3}{4}$ lb pâté brisée (page 18)
2 tablespoons double cream	2 tablespoons heavy cream
GLAZE:	GLAZE:
1 egg yolk	1 egg yolk
1 tablespoon milk	1 tablespoon milk

Peel and quarter the pears, removing the cores, and place in a bowl. Mix together the brandy, sugar and pepper and pour over the pears. Cover and leave to macerate for 3 hours.

Roll out the dough on a floured surface to a rectangle about 1 cm/$\frac{1}{2}$ inch thick. Place on a baking (cookie) sheet. Drain the pears, reserving the juices,

Beignets de fromage blanc; Pithiviers

then pile them up in the centre of the dough. Gather the dough up around the pears to enclose them completely like a parcel. Moisten the edges with water and pinch them together to seal at the top, leaving a 1 cm ($\frac{1}{2}$ inch) hole in the centre.

Beat together the egg yolk and milk for the glaze and brush all over the dough. Bake in a preheated moderately hot oven (200°C/400°F/Gas Mark 6) for 30 minutes.

Remove the *poirat* from the oven and place on a warmed serving platter. Mix together the cream and the reserved juices from the pears, then pour slowly into the *poirat* through the hole in the centre. Serve warm.

SERVES 6

PITHIVIERS

Almond and Puff Pastry Gâteau

This cake takes its name from the town of Pithiviers, 80 kilometres south of Paris, where it was originally created.

Metric/Imperial	American
PÂTE FEUILLETÉE:	PÂTE FEUILLETÉE:
450 g/1 lb plain flour	4 cups all-purpose flour
$\frac{1}{2}$ teaspoon salt	$\frac{1}{2}$ teaspoon salt
450 g/1 lb unsalted butter	2 cups sweet butter
2 teaspoons lemon juice	2 teaspoons lemon juice
about 250 ml/8 fl oz iced water	about 1 cup iced water
ALMOND FILLING:	ALMOND FILLING:
150 g/5 oz butter	$\frac{2}{3}$ cup butter
150 g/5 oz icing sugar, sifted	1 cup sifted confectioner's sugar, firmly packed
2 small eggs, beaten	2 small eggs, beaten
2 tablespoons rum	2 tablespoons rum
150 g/5 oz ground almonds	$1\frac{1}{4}$ cups ground almonds
GLAZE:	GLAZE:
1 egg	1 egg
1 tablespoon water	1 tablespoon water
2 tablespoons icing sugar	2 tablespoons confectioner's sugar

Make the *pâte feuilletée* according to the method on page 19). Chill for 1 hour

For the almond filling, cream the butter in a bowl until soft. Add the icing (confectioner's) sugar and beat until soft, then beat in the eggs and rum. Stir in the ground almonds.

Cut the dough in two, one piece slightly larger than the other. Roll out the larger piece of dough on a floured surface to a circle about 30 cm/12 inches in diameter. Place on a dampened baking (cookie) sheet, then spread the almond filling over the top to within 1 cm/$\frac{1}{4}$ inch of the edge. Brush the edge with water.

Roll out the remaining piece of dough to a circle the same size and place on top of the almond filling. Trim the edges of the dough, press together firmly to seal, then flute with a knife at 1 cm/$\frac{1}{2}$ inch intervals.

Beat together the egg and water for the glaze and brush over the dough. With the point of a knife, score the top of the dough in curves from the centre outwards, like the spokes of a wheel, taking care not to cut right through to the filling.

Bake in a preheated hot oven (220°C/425°F/Gas Mark 7) for 30 minutes until well risen and golden. Remove from the oven, sprinkle the sugar over the cake, then bake for a further 10 minutes. Transfer carefully to a warmed serving platter. Serve warm.

SERVES 8

BEIGNETS DE FROMAGE BLANC

Deep-Fried Cheese Puffs

Metric/Imperial	American
450 g/1 lb fromage blanc★, well drained	2 cups fromage blanc★, well drained
25 g/1 oz caster sugar	2 tablespoons sugar
100 g/4 oz plain flour	1 cup all-purpose flour
2 eggs	2 eggs
oil for deep-frying	oil for deep-frying
caster sugar, for sprinkling	sugar, for sprinkling

Put the cheese in a bowl and beat in the sugar with a wooden spoon until soft and smooth. Stir in the flour a little at a time, beating constantly after each addition. Beat in the eggs one at a time until thoroughly incorporated, then leave the mixture to stand for 1 hour.

Heat the oil in a deep-fat fryer to 190°C/375°F, or until a stale bread cube dropped into the oil turns golden in 10 to 15 seconds. Put teaspoonfuls of the cheese mixture into the hot oil a few at a time and deep-fry for a few minutes until puffed and golden. Remove from the oil with a slotted spoon and drain on kitchen paper towels. Keep warm while frying the remainder.

Pile the cheese puffs in a warmed serving dish and sprinkle with sugar to taste. Serve immediately.

SERVES 6

GLOSSARY

bain marie: A large pan into which a heatproof bowl or pan is placed so that the cooking (in the oven or on top of the stove) is slowed down. This method is necessary for delicate foods such as custards and sauces which would overcook in direct heat.

bleu de bresse: Blue-veined semi-hard cheese made from cow's milk. It is sometimes likened to the Italian gorgonzola.

bouquet garni: Bunch of fresh aromatic herbs (e.g. parsley, thyme and bay leaf, but others can be added) tied together; or crushed, dried herbs contained in a muslin bag, and used to flavour casseroles, stews, soups and stocks.

calf's foot: Added to a slow-cooked dish to give a rich gelatinous gravy. Before adding to the pot, it should be boned, split lengthwise and blanched in boiling water for 3 minutes. A pig's trotter can be used as a substitute.

court-bouillon: Stock acidulated with lemon juice, vinegar or white wine and used for poaching seafood.

croûtons: Small squares of crustless bread fried in butter or equal parts of butter and oil until crisp and golden; used as a garnish for soups.

cèpe mushrooms: One of the more available wild fungi. Can be bought fresh at specialist greengrocers or dried from continental delicatessens (soak for 30 minutes in lukewarm water until they swell to natural size). Use in small quantities only; they have a very strong flavour.

dégorger: To remove strong-flavoured juices from certain vegetables – e.g. aubergines (eggplant) – by salting, then leaving to stand for 15 minutes before rinsing and drying.

desalted anchovies: Fillets which have been drained of oil and left to soak in milk to cover for 20 minutes.

foie gras: Fattened goose liver, a speciality of Alsace. A very expensive delicacy which in cooking can be replaced by pâté de foie gras.

fromage blanc (fromage à la pie): Fresh skimmed cow's milk cheese. Petits suisses (unsalted medium to full fat soft cheese) can be used as a substitute.

goose fat (graisse d'oie): Rendered down fat which has a distinctive flavour. If not available use dripping(s), oil or butter.

Gruyère francais: Rich, matured cow's milk cheese made near the French-Swiss border. Swiss Gruyère can be substituted.

hachis: Finely chopped flavouring mix: e.g. onions or shallots (scallions), garlic, mushrooms or herbs. Can be sprinkled over meat or fish before cooking, or used in a stuffing.

julienne: Food shredded into fine matchstick strips and used as a garnish.

liaisons: Thickening agents for soups, sauces and gravies: e.g. butter and flour (either as a roux or beurre manie, a mixture added in small amounts to the boiling liquid); cornflour (cornstarch) and arrowroot both of which must be blended with water or other liquid; and egg yolks and cream which are mixed together and the hot liquid stirred into them.

marrow bone: Beef or veal leg bone added to many French casseroles, sauces etc. to give a rich thick gravy. Ask the butcher to saw the bone into 5 cm/2 inch rings so the marrow in the middle can be drawn out during cooking, or can be scooped out easily for other use.

moule à manqué: Special French tin used for sponges – it is 5 cm/2 inches deep and has sloping sides.

mouli-légumes: Hand-operated rotary food mill for sieving fruit or vegetables to fine or thick purées.

orange flower water: Essence of the Seville or Bigarade orange. Use it sparingly. Can be bought from pharmacists or delicatessens.

pig's caul: Fatty casing of pig's intestines which has been cleaned and salted (if dry salted it has to be soaked before using). Used to prevent meats such as veal, and pâtés drying out during cooking. May have to be ordered in advance as not commonplace at butchers outside France.

pork rinds: Added to long-cooking casseroles and stews to enrich the gravy. Cut into thin strips and either layer on the base of the dish or arrange on top of the meat and cooking liquid.

roux: A mixture (liaison) of melted butter, or margarine, and flour. Forms the base of certain sauces and thickens them.

saindoux: Rendered down pork back fat, similar to lard. To make, dice or mince the fat, put in heavy-based pan with 7 tablespoons water to each 450 g/1 lb fat and cook over the lowest heat, stirring frequently. Strain into sterilized jars and seal.

spicy sausages: Added to casseroles, stews for extra flavour. French types range from fresh pork (saucisse), to smoked (saucisson), to preserved (saucisson sec). Andouillettes are made from tripe or chitterlings. Choose spiced salami-type sausages if others not available.

vanilla pod (bean): Used whole, halved or split to flavour custards – release flavour by infusing in warmed milk. To make vanilla sugar, leave a halved, split pod (bean) in a jar of caster sugar. Vanilla sugar can also be bought in 25 g/1 oz packets.

zest: The coloured part of citrus peel which can be scraped off finely with the sharp teeth of a gadget called a zester. Or you can use a fine grater, or remove it in strips with a swivel-headed vegetable peeler, then finely chop the strips.

INDEX

ACKNOWLEDGMENTS

The publishers wish to thank the following individuals for their kind permission to use the location photographs in this book:
Robert Golden 9, 12, 17, 18–19; Tessa Traeger 11; Paul Williams 15.

All other photography by Robert Golden and Bryce Attwell. Photographic stylists: Antonia Gaunt and Roisin Neild. Food prepared by Mary Cadogan, Caroline Ellwood and Carole Handslip.

The publishers would also like to express their gratitude to the following companies for the loan of accessories for photography.
Coppershop, 48 Neal St, London WC2; Covent Garden Kitchen Supplies, 3 North Row, The Market, Covent Garden, London WC2; Elizabeth David Ltd, 46 Bourne St, London SW1; Divertimenti, 68 Marylebone Lane, London W1.

The recipes in this book are taken from the Encyclopedia of French Cooking